Forever Honeymoon

Tomeka Lynch Purcell

FOREVER HONEYMOON

B.O.Y. Publications, Inc.
c/o Author Copyrights
P.O. Box 262
Lowell, NC 28098
betonyourselfent.com

Paperback ISBN: 978-1-955605-77-9
Hardback ISBN: 978-1-955605-79-3
Cover and Interior Design: B.O.Y. Enterprises, Inc.

Printed in the United States.

Dedication

To every married woman who has wondered if her marriage is too far gone, may this book help you rediscover your Honeymoon and turn it into Forever.

Table of Contents

Forever: lasting or permanent

Honeymoon: an initial period of enthusiasm or goodwill

Forever Honeymoon:

Lasting or permanent enthusiasm and goodwill

Foreword

Love is a journey—a tapestry woven with shared dreams, moments of laughter, and challenges that test the strength of a bond. For some, this journey feels fleeting, a fleeting spark that dims over time. But for others, love is enduring, like an eternal flame that grows brighter with each passing day. *Forever Honeymoon* is a celebration of that kind of love: the kind that doesn't just endure but thrives, defying the odds, reigniting the spark, and transforming everyday life into an adventure worth savoring.

This book invites you to embrace the magic of a honeymoon that never ends. It's a reminder that love doesn't have to fade; it can deepen, evolve, and enchant in ways you never imagined. Through heartfelt stories, practical wisdom, and tender moments, *Forever Honeymoon* takes you by the hand and shows you how to create a love that feels as fresh and exciting as the day you said, "I do."

Whether you're newly married, celebrating decades together, or simply yearning to renew the passion in your relationship, this book is your guide to keeping love alive and extraordinary. Together, we'll explore what it means to turn ordinary moments into lifelong memories, to rediscover the joy in each other, and to live every day as though it's the start of forever.

Welcome to your *Forever Honeymoon*. Let's make love last a lifetime.

-Real Talk Kim

Disclaimer

Have you ever read a book so full of technical terminology and philosophical debates that you had to use a dictionary to understand what the author was trying to say? Or even worse, you stopped reading after a few pages because, "Girl, what?"

Yeah… this IS NOT one of those. The book you are about to read has been written for the person who wants and needs help but does not enjoy being preached at. So, while you read this book, I want you to imagine we are sitting together on my sofa (or yours if you prefer) with your beverage of choice in hand, and we are having some much-needed sista-to-sista conversations. In some cases, like in the previous sentence, I'm going to use slang because that's the way I speak when I'm talking to my friends. And make no mistake, by picking up this book, you have now become a friend, and I'm going to talk to you like one.

There may also be times I use all caps or extra exclamation points because that's who I am as a person, and I need you to know when I'm lowkey yelling. Oh, and that brings up another point. I'm loud. God gave me volume, and I use it, so be prepared for a bunch of caps. When my girlfriends and I get together, we "kee-kee" loudly!!!

Now that we understand we are just two regular people having a good ole conversation, let's get into it!

-Tomeka

Chapter 1

Understanding Marriage

"Place me like a seal over your heart, like a seal on your arm. For love is as strong as death, its jealousy as enduring as the grave. Love flashes like fire, the brightest kind of flame. Many waters cannot quench love, nor can rivers drown it. If a man tried to buy love with all his wealth, his offer would be utterly scorned." **-Song of Songs 8:6-7 (NLT)**

According to Brittanica.com, marriage is a legally and socially sanctioned union, usually between a man and a woman, that is regulated by laws, rules, customs, beliefs, and attitudes that prescribe the rights and duties of the partners and accord status to their offspring (if any). Now, that's the textbook definition, but let's get one thing straight right out of the gate. As I said in the disclaimer, this is not going to be a stuffy book. So, that's the last stuffy definition you're going to read. From here on out, we are just two people having regular conversations about love, life, and marriage. If you can handle "real talk" laced with love and honesty, you and I are going to get along just fine.

With that being said, let me break down marriage for you in ways you and I both can understand. Marriage is the partnership of a man and woman who wake up each day and choose to love and commit to one another. It is remembering how much you love the person who can't seem to remember to put the toilet seat down. It is showing grace when she leaves her hair in the shower or bundles it all over the bathroom counter. Marriage is staying committed when your frustration wants to tell you to walk away. Marriage is a lesson in forgiveness, patience, and growth. It is the mirror that reveals who we truly are. It is one of the most talked-about subjects on social media: who's getting married, who's getting divorced, who's marriage goals, and everything in between.

Those are some of the more common conversational topics about marriage. But can I tell you a secret, since we're here being open and honest with one another? Marriage is all of those things, but more importantly, a healthy marriage means having someone to walk with you through the darkest moments of your life, seeing you at your absolute worst, and choosing you anyway. Marriage means having someone in the trenches AND on the mountaintop with you. Love, and I'm talking about real love, means having someone who will look you in the eye and say the hard things because they know the truth is what's going to make you free.

The truth is what has sustained my marriage as well as what sparked my desire to write this book. It wasn't pretty, but it was needed, and it was up to me to make the decision to listen to and apply it. As a woman who shows up as a boss in every room she enters, it can be tempting to "boss up" at home, but understanding the true essence of marriage has helped me to understand when it's time to be a boss and when it's time to be a wife. I've learned how to lean into the wisdom my husband shares with me because I don't just want him for a good time; I want him for a lifetime. I am committed to him, he is committed to me, and together, we are committed to this marriage and life we are blessed to enjoy.

Getting back to the truth… One day, my husband had a conversation with me about my weight. Now, he didn't come right out and say, "Tomeka, you need to lose weight." I know we are just getting to know each other, but it's important for you to understand that type of approach would not have worked well for either one of us. Instead, because my husband has my best interest at heart, he told me he wanted to love me at my best.

"What does that even mean?" Does your husband ever decide to be so politically correct that you have no idea what he's trying to say? No… just me? Whatever! Anyway, I asked him to break down what he was trying to say because, of course, my brain had already told me he was trying to say I was fat, and we're married, so he needs to love me no matter what—even if I weigh 250 pounds. Wait… I slipped back into a former thought pattern there. My apologies.

What I meant to explain was that I thought my weight was fine and had an expectation of unconditional love. Now, I know men are visual, but I wrongly believed if he loved me, a few extra pounds shouldn't matter that much. He knows I WORK, A LOT!!! I mean… A LOT, A LOT! By the time I finish working and running all of the businesses, plus helping to care for our family and managing our household, the last thing I feel like doing is working out. My husband, however, goes into our home gym every single morning. No matter what he has going on that day, he prioritizes his health and takes care of it as soon as he wakes up. To him, maintaining the physical appearance that initially attracted me to him was important. He wanted to honor himself by taking care of his health, but he was also trying to honor me.

When he was speaking to me about loving me at my best, what he was really saying was, "I want to see you prioritize your health." But your friend can be a little hardheaded at times, so I didn't get it. Of course, God made sure to drive the point home to me a few days later. I was rushing to get to a meeting on time, and the elevator seemed to be taking too long. I looked and noticed the stairs were right by the elevator. In my mind, it would be easier to just take the stairs since I was only going up one floor. Baaaaby, let me tell you how WRONG I was. That one flight of stairs had me feeling like I needed oxygen and an inhaler, and I don't even have asthma! I had to stop at the top of the stairs to catch my breath because I was completely worn out. And you know how embarrassing it is to be winded, but to be winded AND need to stop and take a break after only one flight of stairs is the WORST!!!

That embarrassment drove home the point my husband was trying to make. While we're far from old, we're also not getting any younger. If I want a long and prosperous life, it starts with my health. It starts with me making a decision to be the very best version of myself. I heard a quote once that says, "How you do one thing is how you do everything." After huffing and puffing to catch my breath, I realized I wasn't giving anything my "best" because I wasn't giving my health my best. My husband was right. I needed to make some changes.

Now, let's be clear. When he said what he said, I had a choice. I could have gotten offended and popped off as only a Black woman could, or I could have chosen to listen to him and hear his heart. It may have taken a winded experience, but I eventually chose the latter, which is what led me to start writing this book. I began to think about how many messages I've seen and heard in pop culture that encourage women to be aggressive, loud, and sassy: messages that leave your ego strengthened, and your marriage weakened. Those messages are like bad programming that continues to rip away at the fibers of marriage. I want to offer a different message, one that gives tools, insights, and support for men and women who desire partnership, love, and commitment with the same person for the rest of their lives. I know this is possible because I have the honor of living it, and with God's grace, my husband and I will do so until our dying breath.

Realistic Expectations

Truly understanding what marriage is and what it isn't begins with setting realistic expectations. Many people grew up watching terrible marriages that were toxic and traumatic or with fairytales they saw on television. It's very rare to find a person who was fortunate enough to grow up with an example of a healthy marriage in their home. Because of this, we often come into marriages with unrealistic and unspoken expectations of the union, our spouse, and ourselves. Unspoken expectations are always a recipe for disaster, but when you are secretly hoping for some unrealistic fantasy, the odds of you being happy in the marriage drop significantly. Throw in the current social media trends and couples challenges, and the whole thing turns into one big dumpster fire!

So, what are realistic expectations for your specific marriage? Girl, I don't know!!!! But here's the thing: you and your spouse have the opportunity to define that for yourselves. The deeper you grow in your connection and understanding of each other, the easier it will be to set realistic expectations. The more you know about each other, the more you will grow as a couple. Try not to hold on to the fantasy of what you hoped marriage would be. Instead, embrace the truth of what your marriage can be.

You may never have the Instagram aesthetic in your home, but can the two of you create a space that is full of love, honor, respect, joy, and peace? You may never have the bank account that allows you to fly around on private jets, but can the two of you go for a drive after dinner and just vibe together? You may never be in a position to live off of one income, but can you learn to make the time you spend together memorable? Can you appreciate what you have versus crying over what you feel is missing? Sometimes, a simple shift in perspective is all we need to feel more complete in our marriages.

Am I saying you should settle? Really? Did you just ask me that? Since we are still early in this book, I'm going to give you a pass, but do me a favor real quick. Stop and go look at the cover of this book. Go ahead, hold your place on this page, close the book, and stare at the front cover. Do you see settle anywhere on there? The answer is no because I don't believe in settling. I'll work three jobs and sleep when I'm dead before I settle for less than what I want and deserve. So, no. I'm not suggesting you should settle. I'm telling you to focus on what is really important, put aside childish, vague, and pointless trends, and talk to your spouse about what you need to feel valued, loved, supported, and heard in your marriage.

Establishing realistic boundaries creates balance and harmony within the home. This helps to ensure both of your needs and desires are being met. If you haven't done so already, set aside time to discuss expectations in every area of your life and marriage. What do you need to feel supported around the house with chores, cooking, paying bills, caring for the children, etc.? How do you and your spouse feel about working outside of the home? How often do you both need sex? How many date nights do you need per month?

Far too many couples get distracted by chasing the next goal or taking care of responsibilities, but few sit down and discuss what they are willing to do to accomplish those goals. Here's a phrase you are going to see me repeat in this book: Never let your marriage become a casualty of your ambition. Prioritize setting proper expectations so that you both are very clear about what needs to happen and when.

Commitment to Compromise

Why should couples commit to compromising in their marriage? Because compromise is the glue that holds the greater good of the union together. It's the decision, day after day, to prioritize the health of the relationship over individual preferences. Let's face it:

no marriage is perfect, and expecting otherwise is a surefire way to set yourself up for disappointment. Instead, thriving couples learn to embrace the imperfections, roll with the ups and downs, and choose to work as a team—even when it's hard. Compromise isn't about "giving in" or "losing" to your spouse; it's about building something stronger together.

Marriage is a partnership, and no partnership works if one person is always taking and the other is always giving. Both people must be prepared to navigate the valleys as much as they celebrate the peaks. This means accepting that there will be disagreements, frustrations, and times when your needs and your spouse's needs don't align perfectly. Compromise is what bridges that gap. It's what allows you to navigate those moments without tearing each other apart. Instead of seeing it as a sacrifice of your wants, think of compromise as an investment in the relationship—a decision to prioritize "us" over "me."

Sacrifice is a word that doesn't get enough attention in modern conversations about marriage, but it's vitally important on both sides. There will be times when you have to put your spouse's needs above your own—not because you're losing, but because you're choosing love. Maybe that looks like giving up a weekend trip with friends because your spouse needs your support at home. Or maybe it's about letting go of being "right" in an argument to restore peace in your relationship. These aren't losses; they're love in action. When both partners are willing to make sacrifices, the relationship becomes a safe and sacred space where both people feel valued and secure.

Part of compromise is being ready for change and, more importantly, being okay with changing yourself. Marriage has a way of revealing parts of us we didn't even know needed work—selfishness, impatience, pride. It's humbling, but it's also an opportunity for growth. Commitment in marriage means saying, "I'm in this for life, no matter how many things I have to change about myself for the good of this relationship." It's not about changing who you are at your core but being willing to grow, adapt, and let go of habits or behaviors that don't serve your marriage. That kind of commitment takes humility, but it also builds intimacy and trust.

Change can be scary because it requires vulnerability. It means admitting that you don't have all the answers and that there's room for improvement. But here's the thing: when both partners are willing to change for the sake of the relationship, it creates a beautiful cycle of growth. You're not just working on yourselves as individuals—you're growing together as a couple. We'll talk more about growth later, but just know: every compromise, every adjustment, and every sacrifice becomes a brick in the foundation of your marriage, making it stronger and more resilient with each passing year.

Being in tune with your spouse is another key part of compromise. You can't make sacrifices or adjustments for the good of the relationship if you don't know what your spouse truly needs. That's why communication is so important. It's about more than just listening—it's about understanding. Pay attention to what works and what doesn't in your marriage. Learn your spouse's love language, their triggers, hopes, and fears. The more in tune you are, the better equipped you'll be to navigate challenges together.

There's a beautiful balance in compromise. It's not about one person always giving and the other always taking; it's about creating harmony. Some days, you'll sacrifice for your spouse, and other days, they'll sacrifice for you. However, in a healthy marriage, both people are willing to lay down their wants for the good of the collective. That mutual commitment builds trust and fosters a deep sense of security. You know your spouse has your back, and they know you have theirs. And that's what allows a marriage to thrive.

Compromise isn't always easy. There will be times when it feels uncomfortable, inconvenient, or downright unfair. But the rewards are worth it. Every time you choose the good of the marriage over your own preferences, you're planting seeds of love, trust, and connection. Over time, those seeds grow into a marriage that is strong, resilient, and deeply fulfilling.

Marriage is a journey, and compromise is the vehicle that moves you forward. It's not about keeping score or making sure everything is perfectly equal—it's about making sure both people feel loved, respected, and valued. When you approach compromise with a willing heart and a focus on the greater good, it stops feeling like a chore and starts feeling like an act of love. And that's what marriage is all about: choosing love every single day.

Why Forever Honeymoon?

The honeymoon is often viewed as the happiest time of the marriage. It's the time when the couple is away from the world, enjoying a fantastic vacation and all the sex their bodies can handle. Let's be real, who isn't having great sex on vacation? There are no bills, children, household chores, work stress, or in-laws to be upset about—just two people in love enjoying each other. But what happens when that same couple returns home, and the stress of everyday life begins to take a toll on their communication and patience? Do they just abandon all the joy they shared on the honeymoon?

Sadly, this is what happens in many relationships. Too often, couples approach marriage with a cultural viewpoint that the honeymoon won't last forever, and eventually, they'll be irritated and arguing with each other. But what if that didn't have to be the case? What if you can return from vacation and spend the rest of your life showing your spouse the same love, respect, and patience you showed them in the beginning? What if you committed to showing up in your marriage every day as the best possible version of yourself, regardless of what is going on around you? Sound impossible or unrealistic?

Well, let me make it plain for you. Expectation frames your reality. It is never okay to set unrealistic expectations for anyone, including yourself. However, deciding to work on yourself to be the healthiest you've ever been in your emotions, physical body, mind, and spirit is not unrealistic. In fact, every "difficult" thing you have ever overcome started with your decision to be better—a refusal to accept what was being presented to you. When it comes to your marriage, that decision is the breeding ground for your expectations. If you expect a difficult marriage, you will have a difficult marriage. On the other hand, if you expect a *Forever Honeymoon* and do the work, you'll have a *Forever Honeymoon.*

What does a *Forever Honeymoon* marriage look like to you? Use the space below to explain the type of marriage you desire. Remember, your expectation is your foundation. Be intentional and realistic!

_____

_____

_____

_____

_____

_____

_____

_____

_____

_____

_____

_____

_____

_____

_____

_____

_____

_____

_____

_____

_____

_____

_____

_____

Chapter 2

Communication: The Heartbeat of Marriage

"Communication is always easy when you're right. The tough part is learning to continue communicating even when you're wrong."

Communication is one of the most important tools every couple needs to develop. Growth will not happen in your marriage until you learn how to communicate effectively. It just won't. I know someone told you if you didn't have anything nice to say, it was best not to say anything at all, but that was advice for a child. You are a full-grown adult doing life with another full-grown adult! It's time for you to learn how to say what you need to say in a way your spouse will be able to hear, understand, and receive. Not saying anything because you don't have anything nice to say might fly in elementary school, but in marriage, it's called the silent treatment. And if you're not careful, it can quietly erode the connection you've worked so hard to build.

Healthy communication doesn't mean you'll never argue or that every conversation will be smooth sailing. It means learning how to engage with each other in ways that strengthen your bond instead of tearing it down. It means developing the tools to navigate hard conversations, express your feelings honestly, and truly hear each other's hearts. Communication isn't just about what you say—it's about how you say it, how you listen, and how you respond. And like any skill, it takes practice, patience, and intention.

One of the first and most important skills you need to master is active listening. Let me ask you something: When your spouse is talking, are you really listening, or are you just waiting for your turn to speak? Be honest with yourself here. Too often, we listen to respond rather than to understand. We're already crafting our rebuttal or getting ready to defend our point of view instead of focusing on what our partner is actually saying. But here's the truth: Your spouse needs to feel heard before they'll feel understood. And when they feel understood, a real connection happens.

Active listening requires you to slow down and give your full attention to what your spouse is saying. That means putting down your phone, turning off the TV, and maintaining eye contact. It also means asking clarifying questions, like "What I hear you saying is…" or "Can you help me understand that a little more?" These small shifts show your spouse that you're not just hearing their words—you're hearing their heart. Listening to understand is a game-changer because it validates your spouse's feelings and creates a safe space for honest conversation.

But let's not stop there. Listening is only one side of the equation. The other side is learning how to express your own feelings and needs honestly and respectfully. This is where many couples struggle because it requires vulnerability. It's not easy to say, "I'm hurt," or "I need more support from you," especially when you're worried about how your spouse might respond. But avoiding the conversation doesn't make the issue go away—it just makes it fester.

When you're expressing your feelings, the key is to focus on "I" statements rather than "you" statements. For example, instead of saying, "You never listen to me," try, "I feel unheard when we're talking, and that's hard for me." The difference is subtle but powerful. "You" statements often come across as accusations, which can put your spouse on the defensive. "I" statements, on the other hand, focus on your experience and invite understanding rather than conflict.

Respect is also crucial. You can be honest without being harsh. There's a way to say what you need to say without tearing your spouse down. Proverbs 15:1 says, "A gentle answer turns away wrath, but a harsh word stirs up anger." The way you deliver your message matters just as much as the message itself. Think about the tone you're using and the words you're choosing. Are they building up your marriage or creating distance?

While we're on the subject of honesty, let's talk about the importance of regular check-ins. Life gets busy, and it's easy to go days—or even weeks—without having a real conversation. You might be sharing a home, a bed, and a calendar, but if you're not intentionally checking in with each other, you risk losing the connection that holds your marriage together. Regular check-ins are like a pulse check for your relationship. They give you both a chance to share what's on your heart, address any concerns, and reconnect.

Daily check-ins don't have to be long or formal. It could be as simple as sitting down together for 10 minutes at the end of the day to ask, "How was your day? How are you feeling?" Weekly check-ins might be a little more intentional—a time to talk about your goals, your schedule, or anything that's been on your mind. These moments of connection help you stay on the same page and catch small issues before they become big problems. They also remind your spouse that you care about what's happening in their world.

Now, let's get real for a minute. No matter how well you communicate, you're going to disagree. It's inevitable. You're two different people with different perspectives, and that's okay. In fact, it's healthy. Disagreements are a natural part of any relationship. The goal isn't to avoid them—it's to learn how to disagree well.

Disagreeing well means fighting fair. It means focusing on the issue at hand rather than dragging up past grievances or attacking your spouse's character. It means staying calm and respectful even when emotions are running high. This is easier said than done, especially when you feel hurt or frustrated. But remember: Winning an argument at the expense of your spouse's feelings isn't really a win. The goal isn't to win—it's to resolve the issue in a way that strengthens your marriage.

One way to disagree well is to take a break when things get too heated. If you find yourself raising your voice or saying things you don't mean, hit the pause button. Step away, take a few deep breaths, and come back to the conversation when you're both calmer. It's okay to say, "I need a moment to collect my thoughts so I can approach this conversation with love and respect." Taking a break doesn't mean you're avoiding the issue—it means you're prioritizing the health of your marriage.

It's also important to stay solution-focused. Instead of dwelling on the problem, work together to find a way forward. Ask yourselves, "What's the best outcome for us as a team? How can we compromise or collaborate to move past this?" Disagreements don't have to drive a wedge between you. When handled with care, they can actually bring you closer together by deepening your understanding of each other's needs and perspectives.

As you work on communication, don't forget to give yourselves grace. Nobody gets this perfectly right all the time. There will be moments when you speak out of turn, fail to listen or say something you regret. When that happens, own it. Apologize, forgive, and move forward. Marriage isn't about perfection—it's about progress. Every conversation is an opportunity to learn, grow, and love each other better.

Communication isn't always easy, but it's worth it. It's the bridge that connects your hearts, the tool that resolves your conflicts, and the glue that holds your marriage together. As you learn to listen actively, express yourself honestly, check in regularly, and disagree well, you'll build a foundation of trust and intimacy that will carry your relationship through anything life throws your way.

So, start today. Have that conversation you've been avoiding. Listen a little more closely. Ensure your words are wrapped in love and kindness. And watch as your marriage begins to grow in ways you never thought possible. The grass is greener where you water it. Water your marriage with communication, care, concern, and support. Communication is a skill, and like any skill, it gets easier with practice. Keep showing up, keep learning, and keep loving. Your marriage is worth it.

Simple Communication Tips

1. Be willing to mold what you want to say so that it will be easier for the hearer to accept it.
2. It's okay to disagree but agree to collectively decide how to move forward.
3. Practice active listening. Listen to understand, not just respond.
4. Remember, the goal is to come to an agreement. Be careful about which hills you're willing to die on.
5. Sometimes, you need to connect with your spouse sexually before completing a conversation. The emotional, physical, and spiritual connection that happens during sex helps you both remember what you are fighting for and takes the edge off of your frustration.
6. Express your feelings and needs honestly and respectfully.
7. Communicate humbly and transparently at all times.
8. Actively look for a solution you both can live with. The goal is always forever!
9. Practice daily check-ins. "Honey, how was your day?"
10. Instead of planning to argue, plan to find common ground.

Forever Moments

Now that you've read the chapter, use the space below to create a communication plan.

Topic that needs to be discussed:

_____

_____

What is most important to you about this topic?

_____

_____

_____

What do you want your partner to know about your feelings around this topic?

_____

_____

_____

What is your ideal outcome?

_____

_____

_____

Where are you willing to compromise?

_____

_____

_____

You know your spouse; when is the best time to approach this subject?

_____

_____

_____

Chapter 3

Conflict Resolution

"The ending is not your business." -Pastor Kim Jones

Now, friend, the story I am about to tell you will not make me look good, but if you learn from my mistakes, it can save your marriage, and that is why you're reading this book, right? Okay, so here it goes. When I married my husband, he did not have any biological children, but I had three. For many years, I was a single mom who made all of the decisions concerning the children. I was the decision-maker, their confidante, the disciplinarian, and everything in between. I was the be-all-end-all, and the buck always stopped with me. I love my children with everything within me, and while I wanted a husband, I did not initially consider how having a husband would impact how I raised my children.

In the early years of our marriage, my views regarding the children were a huge point of contention. When a situation would arise and my husband did not agree with the decision I was making, I'd say to him, "You don't have kids, so you don't understand." Now that I'm typing this, I'm hearing how terrible it sounds, but don't start judging me now. I've lived, and I've learned, so my current responses are much more appropriate. But in the beginning, I did not want my husband to help me raise the children, and it almost cost me my marriage.

I'd been a single mother for so long that I operated on autopilot most of the time. It never occurred to me that getting married meant I had to consider another person's opinion when it came to my children. Truthfully, I didn't consider that getting married meant they would no longer be MY children; they would become OUR children. I wanted a marriage, but I did not count the cost of what it would look like to add a husband to the mix of parenting.

My husband was patient with me at first, but after a couple of years, he put his foot down, and I had a decision to make. Either I was going to learn how to resolve conflict properly and include him in ALL decision-making, or we were going to get a divorce. Listen, I love that man, and I wanted him forever, so I had to suck it up and learn how to resolve the parenting conflicts in a healthier way.

The first thing I had to do was learn to trust the man I married. He wasn't sent as an answer to my prayer just to be my husband; he was also sent to help me raise the children. I had to respect God's decision to assign my husband to all of our lives. I had to realize I had been the only one to make the decisions, but that wasn't God's design for my life. God never intended for me to be a single mother, so He sent a man into my life to help me carry the parenting load.

Next, I had to recognize my husband's inclination to step back instead of inserting himself in situations regarding the children didn't mean he didn't care about the choices being made or the outcome. Instead, he was giving the children and me space to adjust to his presence. He's more reserved than I am and far less likely to get rowdy when he doesn't like something. I had to learn his silence didn't mean acceptance. I had to be open to slowing down and allowing him to be a part of the process and eventually my partner in parenting.

Finally, I had to acknowledge the issue wasn't really the thing we weren't agreeing on. The issue was me not realizing we were on the same team. I was isolating and freezing my partner out without realizing it. Again, my nature is to be more vocal and proactive, while that man of mine is as relaxed and laid back as they come. The loudest person in the room can sometimes feel as though they are right because they are being heard. I had to realize being right was not about being heard; it was about making space for my husband's voice, opinions, and thoughts. In our home, we don't live by the phrase "happy wife, happy life"; we live by "happy spouse, happy house."

Now, when we disagree, we listen to each other and work to hear each other's heart. He wants to make me happy, and I want to make him happy. We recognize we are on the same team with the same end goal, so instead of biting each other's head off, we address issues promptly so they won't fester into something much larger than they need to be. Issues are birthed out of differing opinions that are allowed to grow into unresolved arguments. Arguments by nature bring out the worst in us. Now you begin to harp on who is right or who is wrong rather than focusing on what you really need to resolve.

In a marriage, it's always important to focus on a solution that you both can live with. Stop making hills you are willing to die on. I mean… why would you want to die when you can live, and in harmony at that!? Let your pride go and be quick to apologize. Resolving the issue is far more important than your pride. The enemy is out to steal, kill, and destroy, but you have the biggest mediator in the game on your side: the Holy Spirit!

Another powerful conflict resolution tool is practicing empathy. This just means seeing things from your spouse's perspective. I know you've only seen out of your own eyes your whole life, but be intentional about trying to see where your spouse is coming from. You have different backgrounds and experiences for a reason. God brought you two together to make your lives better, not to make you a clone of each other. There is beauty in seeing from a different perspective, and what better perspective than the person you married?

The bottom line is, no one wants to be in conflict in their marriage, but most people do not know how to respond when their spouse isn't in the best mood. Like everything else, the mood of the home flows from the head down. If the head comes home in a bad mood, you can trust and believe the mood of the whole house will shift. If you're not careful, something that had nothing to do with you can turn into a huge conflict.

I noticed this was happening in our marriage, so I started practicing actively pouring into my husband from the moment he walks in the door. Even when I'm not having a good day, I do my best to see things from his perspective and contribute to turning the day around for both of us. No matter how busy I am when he comes home, I do my best to stop, greet him, and let him know I'm happy he's home. If the call I'm on is not absolutely necessary, it's a wrap as soon as that man walks through the door.

I'm not saying I'm perfect because ya girl is human, and sometimes it takes a minute to turn off work mode, but I am aware of his need to be acknowledged when he comes home, and I enjoy filling that need for him. Just that simple change in our routine, me switching from boss to wife when he comes home, has resolved conflict in our marriage. Not everything has to remain a point of contention when both of you are willing to do the work to resolve the issues.

I studied my spouse to find out what works for him, and I believe he studied me. We recognize each other's needs and prioritize them. And you know what happened? Things that used to trip us up stopped tripping us up! It's hard to stay mad at someone who has spent the last week putting you first. We have spent so much time loving each other well that when we do fall short or disagree, there's no knock-down, drag-out argument or talks of divorce. Instead, there is kindness and understanding because at the end of the day, we both understand we are in this thing FOREVER!

Now, real quick before we change the subject, let's talk about two things that will try to destroy your forever: dirty fighting and comparison! No matter how many times you say you're sorry, words can never be unheard once you've spoken them. So, even when you are upset and unsure if you like your spouse, WATCH YOUR MOUTH!!! Your spouse is on your team. Why would you ever want to break them down with your words? When they lose, you lose! What you say and the way you say it matters, even when you are pissed!

Instead of plotting your next comeback lines in the mirror when you are mad at your spouse, allow the Holy Spirit to season your words before you speak. For those of you who may not know what that means, ask God to help you speak to your spouse in a way that they can receive. Then, actually, LISTEN when He responds and follow His instructions! The thing you feel like you just "have to" say is more than likely your emotions attempting to sabotage your relationship. Don't listen to them because if you push that man away, those same emotions will have you stalking him when he leaves!

ISSA SET UP SIS! DON'T FALL FOR IT!

When tensions are not high, sit down with your spouse and agree on fair fighting rules. Decide which topics are off-limits during arguments. Abandon name-calling because what are you doing calling people names at your big age, anyway? You and I both know you know better! Learn how to express your disappointment, hurt, or frustration without continuing the cycle of toxicity and destructive communication. A wise woman builds her spouse up; a foolish woman cuts off her own nose to spite her face. I know I don't have to tell you which one you are, right?

Unresolved conflicts are breeding grounds for the enemy, so instead of holding on to your anger, make up with your spouse quickly! Some other woman is saying, "Hey sexy," when he walks by at work while you are at home giving him the silent treatment is a bad look. Again, don't be foolish, Sis. Someone is waiting in the wings whispering, "He's a good man, Savannah." Don't leave space for her to move from the wings to under his wing!

Ensure you and your home are your husband's sanctuary. You want to create an atmosphere of peace and love in your home. No one wants to come home to strife and hostility. Your husband was sent by God to be your covering. It's your job to work with him and allow yourself to be covered. Remember, an umbrella in the trunk of your car does you no good when you walk out of the salon with that gorgeous silk press and the sky decides to open up. In that situation, you'd technically have something to protect you and your hair from the elements, but you chose to walk away from it. The same is true for your husband. If he's attempting to cover and protect you, but you choose to walk away from his protection, not only do you run the risk of harm, you undermine his assignment in your life.

Be willing to listen and follow his lead. If you can't follow him, why did you marry him? Even unbelievers understand the husband should be the head of the home. You became HIS Mrs., not the other way around.

Anger doesn't just appear out of thin air. It often feels like it, especially in the heat of the moment, but there's always a deeper reason behind it. When you or your spouse feel angry, it's important to pause and recognize that this emotion likely stems from an unmet need, a hurt feeling, or even a buildup of stress. It could be something as simple as feeling unappreciated after a long day or as complex as an ongoing issue that hasn't been addressed properly.

The key is to realize that anger is often a surface-level response to something much deeper. It's not just about the immediate trigger—like forgetting to take out the trash or being late to an event—it's about the underlying emotions or frustrations that have been building up over time.

Instead of letting anger escalate into a full-blown argument, couples should take the time to explore the root cause together. Ask yourselves: What's really going on here? What's the underlying issue that needs to be addressed? By discussing the root cause calmly and openly, you can work together to resolve the deeper issue without turning it into a confrontation. Remember, the goal isn't to "win" or prove a point—it's to understand each other better and strengthen your relationship. When you shift your focus from arguing over the symptoms to addressing the root cause, you create space for healing, growth, and a deeper emotional connection.

Comparison Breeds Unnecessary Conflict

A major and underdiscussed cause of conflict in marriage is comparison. Stop comparing your marriage to the next-door neighbors' or your husband's friend and his wife, or even your parents. Understand that most of the time when you are seeing them, you are only getting the good parts, not the nights they were arguing and one of them left the house to stay at a hotel. You have no idea about how rough it was for them when the bills were piling up and neither of them could figure out the next move, so they took it out on each other. And don't get me started on the highlight reel we call social media. Half of last year's #relationshipgoals are already divorced!

Stop sitting around getting angry, comparing your marriage to someone else's, when you have no idea how their marriage really is. Instead of comparing what your husband does for you to what your friend's husband does for her, start focusing on how you can water your own marriage. The grass isn't greener at your neighbor's house because they are better than you. It's greener because they water it, PERIOD! So, stop tripping and get your water hose out. And if you're really about that life, let your husband bring the hose and you provide the water…if you know, you know!

Understand that your marriage is different, but it is the exact thing that was meant for you both. Small words can soften a situation and allow intimacy back in. For example, "I promise I don't like you right now, but those pants look good on you," can quickly break the tension during a conflict. Attraction can be stronger when strife is present IF you decide to focus on what you have instead of what you think someone else has. Use it to find your way back to each other. Know that everything is not always as it seems. Focus on your partner and their needs (not yours), and you will soon replace the bitterness and anger with schoolgirl laughs and inappropriate/appropriate thoughts when your man walks by. Trust me and try it.

Conflict Resolution Plan

Okay Sis, now that we have agreed not to plan our next argument in the mirror, let's plan to be healthy in our conflict resolution. Use the space the below to write down a few conflict resolution strategies for your relationship.

_____

_____

_____

_____

_____

_____

_____

_____

_____

_____

_____

_____

_____

_____

_____

_____

Chapter 4

Spending Quality Time Together

"The most valuable commodity you will ever spend is time."

I heard a story years ago about a successful businesswoman who was asked during the last year of her life what she wished she'd done differently. To put things into perspective, this woman achieved every business goal she set her mind to, made great philanthropic strides, raised children who went on to be successful in life, and remained married to the love of her life until he died 15 years before she was being interviewed. Her life, by all standards, had been very well lived. She said she'd been asked that same question several times before, and her answer this time was going to be different. Now that she realized her own was nearing its end, she said the one thing she would do differently if given the chance to live her life again would be to spend more quality time with her husband. He'd died unexpectedly, and they'd always believed they had more time to travel and enjoy retirement together. Instead, he'd died in his sleep two years after retiring. The elderly woman said she felt robbed of the time she longed to spend with the one who made her feel like the prettiest woman in every room they entered.

Like most productive adults, my time is extremely valuable to me. When you run multiple businesses, take care of yourself, your family, and your home, the last thing you want to waste is your time. If we're not intentional about the way we spend our time, we can go weeks without spending quality time with the person we pledged to spend the rest of our lives with. What good would it be for me to spend all of my time building a future legacy while my present blessing is being placed on the back burner? God willing, my schedule will always be demanding, and there will always be projects that require my time. This is where the importance of prioritization and intentionality come into play. My marriage is the most valuable Earthly relationship I have. I don't just want to give my husband my time. I want to spend quality time connecting with him in ways that fill us both up emotionally, physically, spiritually, and mentally.

Being the best wife I can be to my husband is non-negotiable. The same way I schedule meetings and other work-related tasks, I am intentional about scheduling time with my husband. On occasion, this may look like he and I eating breakfast together. Other days, we may eat lunch or dinner together. I create a routine that allows us to be together as much as possible. I recognize there are times our schedules will require us to be in separate spaces, but my intention is for those times to be few and far between. My goal is to spend as much quality time with him as humanly possible.

The obligations we have cannot be neglected, so there will be seasons of your marriage that you cannot spend 10-15 solid hours together every day. There may be times that you only have 1-2 hours. This is why we must also be intentional about the quality of the time spent over the quantity. When things are in abundant supply, it can be very easy to neglect them for fear it will always be there. When the supply is reduced, it creates a sense of urgency. If your schedule is JAM PACKED like mine, I want you to see time with your spouse the same way. There is a limited supply of time, so you must urgently ensure you use that time to connect intimately with your spouse. No… that was not permission or a suggestion for midday quickies. I know some of you thought that. If that's your jam, have at it. But, just so we're clear, that's not what I was suggesting. We'll discuss intimacy in a later chapter, but for now let's just say, some of the most intimate moments with your spouse will happen when you both are fully clothed. They happen when you are both fully engaged in the moment and emotionally transparent and vulnerable. Those moments build what is unseen with your physical eye and lay the foundation for unbridled passion. It's the moment when two hearts truly become one. Those are the moments you will look back on for the rest of your lives because they are the seeds of deep abiding love, and they do not require 15 hours of free time. Now, let's go deeper…

Balancing Personal Space with Togetherness

Marriage is a beautiful blend of two lives coming together, but it also involves maintaining a balance between togetherness and the need for personal space. This balance is vital for the health of the relationship. Just because you're married doesn't mean you stop being individuals with your own interests, hobbies, or need for time to recharge. On the other hand, spending quality time together as a couple is equally important for nurturing connection and intimacy. Finding the right balance between personal space and togetherness is essential to create a thriving marriage where both partners feel loved, supported, and fulfilled.

One of the most common misconceptions about marriage is that couples must spend all their time together to have a strong bond. While spending time with your spouse is incredibly important, constantly being in each other's space without any room for individuality can sometimes lead to feelings of frustration or overwhelm. On the flip side, too much independence can make your relationship feel distant or disconnected. So, how do you strike that delicate balance? Let's explore how to honor both the need for personal space and the importance of shared time as a couple.

Understanding the Need for Personal Space

Personal space in a marriage is not about wanting to be away from your partner or avoiding connection. Instead, it's about recognizing that both partners have individual needs that may require time apart to recharge, pursue personal interests, or reflect. God designed us all uniquely, and part of what makes a relationship vibrant is each partner's individuality. Having time for yourself allows you to reconnect with who you are, reflect on your personal goals, and engage in activities that refresh your spirit.

Personal space might look different for everyone. For some, it's quiet time alone to pray, meditate, or read. For others, it's time spent pursuing a hobby, exercising, or meeting up with friends. The key is to understand what personal space means for both you and your spouse and to communicate openly about it. When you give each other the freedom to step away from the shared space of marriage for a bit, you allow room for personal growth, and that, in turn, enriches the relationship.

If one partner craves more alone time than the other, it's essential to have conversations about expectations. For example, you could say, "I love spending time with you, but I also need some quiet time to recharge. It helps me show up as my best self when we're together." Framing the conversation this way communicates that the desire for personal space isn't about pulling away emotionally—it's about refilling your energy tank so you can continue to pour love into the relationship.

Friend, that man loves you, but he needs personal space too!

Having personal space in marriage can actually strengthen your relationship in several ways. First, it helps prevent feelings of suffocation or burnout. Even in the closest of marriages, it's natural for partners to need time to themselves. Without that space, resentment or frustration can start to build, leading to tension.

Personal space also allows each partner to continue growing as an individual. It's important to remember that before you became "us," you were two separate people with your own interests, dreams, and passions. Maintaining some of that individuality keeps the relationship dynamic and exciting because it allows each person to bring new experiences and growth back into the marriage.

Another benefit is that personal space can make your time together even more meaningful. Absence, even in small doses, truly does make the heart grow fonder. When you've had a little time apart, you can come back together with fresh energy, more appreciation for each other, and often, new things to talk about or share. Instead of feeling like you're constantly around each other, which can sometimes lead to taking each other for granted, personal space creates a healthy rhythm in the relationship.

While personal space is essential, it's equally important to nurture togetherness. Marriage thrives on connection, intimacy, and shared experiences. Creating intentional time to be together strengthens your bond and reminds you why you chose each other in the first place. Togetherness in a marriage isn't just about being in the same room—it's about truly connecting. This could mean setting aside time each week for a date night, even if it's something simple like cooking dinner together or taking a walk around the neighborhood. It's about having moments where you're fully present with each other, free from distractions like phones, work, or household chores.

Sometimes, togetherness can be as simple as sharing a cup of coffee in the morning or praying together at the end of the day. The key is to make these moments intentional. When you prioritize time together, even amidst busy schedules, it communicates that your marriage is a priority and that you value your connection as a couple.

Physical affection is another important aspect of togetherness. Regular physical touch—whether it's holding hands, hugging, or simply sitting close together—releases oxytocin, the "love hormone," which fosters feelings of closeness and emotional safety. Even when life gets hectic, making time for physical affection can keep the bond between you and your spouse strong.

The balance between personal space and togetherness looks different for every couple, and it often changes over time. What works in one season of your marriage might need adjusting in another. In other words, I know y'all used to do everything together, but that man might need to come up for air from time to time, and that does not mean he loves you any less. It just means it's time for you to find something you enjoy doing too, so that you both find personal fulfillment and enjoyment.

So, how can we do that while also maintaining our intimate connection? I'm so glad you asked, friend. I listed some practical tips below, and I broke them down so you can read through them faster. Do me a favor though, don't just read them to get to the next chapter. Promise me you'll actually implement them so you and that man can get more quality time in. I want to see y'all win!

Alright, here we go…

1. Communicate Your Needs:

Open and honest communication is crucial. Talk to your spouse about what personal space means to you, and listen to what it means to them. This could include setting aside time for individual activities, like reading or going for a solo walk and making sure your partner understands that this is about self-care, not distancing yourself from the relationship.

2. Respect Each Other's Boundaries:

Respecting your spouse's need for space without feeling hurt or rejected is important. For example, if your partner wants some alone time to unwind after work, respect that boundary without taking it personally. Trust that this time apart will make your time together even more valuable.

3. Create a Routine for Togetherness:

Just as you carve out time for personal space, it's essential to schedule regular time for togetherness. Whether it's a weekly date night, daily devotional time, or a weekend activity, having consistent rituals that bring you together helps keep your relationship strong and ensures you stay connected.

4. Be Flexible and Understanding:

There will be seasons when one partner needs more space, such as during a particularly stressful time at work or when dealing with a personal challenge. Being flexible and understanding in these moments helps create a sense of safety in the relationship. Likewise, there may be times when your spouse needs more togetherness to feel secure or connected. Being attuned to each other's needs and willing to adapt will go a long way in maintaining balance.

5. Enjoy Solo and Shared Hobbies:

Having individual hobbies and shared interests can create a healthy balance between personal space and togetherness. Encourage each other to pursue hobbies independently—whether it's painting, cycling, or reading—while also finding activities you both enjoy. This way, you're both nurturing your personal growth while also creating opportunities to bond.

6. Pray Together and Separately:

As Christian couples, prayer is a powerful way to both nurture togetherness and respect personal space. Praying together as a couple strengthens your spiritual connection and invites God into your relationship. At the same time, spending time in personal prayer allows you to reflect on your own walk with God, which enhances your individual spiritual growth and enables you to be a stronger partner in the marriage.

Balancing personal space with togetherness takes practice, but it can be done. By allowing room for each partner to recharge, pursue personal interests, and grow as individuals, you foster a relationship that respects and celebrates your unique identities. At the same time, nurturing intentional moments of connection and shared experiences strengthens your bond and reinforces the love that brought you together.

Remember, your marriage is a partnership, and part of that partnership is knowing when to come together and when to give each other room to BREATHE! With open communication, mutual respect, and a shared commitment to growing both individually and as a couple, you can create a marriage that is balanced, loving, and resilient.

Chapter 5

Intimacy- The Blood of Your Marriage

I want you to imagine your marriage as its own separate body for a moment. You and your spouse have become one. This new body has been formed from all of who you are and all of whom your spouse is, and it has been merged together into one living, thinking, feeling, and growing body. Like any other body, your marriage "body" is going to require a vehicle to keep all parts of it well-nourished and thriving. In a physical body, that vehicle is blood.

Blood carries oxygen, nutrients, and hormones throughout the body. If, for some reason, whether it be by trauma or other injury, blood stops flowing to an area of the body, that body part will die. If the body as a whole loses too much blood, the body will die. The blood that sustains your marriage "body" is intimacy. Intimacy is the vehicle that delivers oxygen and nutrients to the heart of your marriage, weaving together moments of joy, vulnerability, compassion, and love. It creates unspoken bonds that will create a magnetic-like attraction so that even in the toughest of times, you and your spouse will be drawn toward each other.

Just as your natural body cannot live without blood, your marriage "body" cannot live without intimacy. Intimacy must be nurtured to ensure the blood continues to flow to every area of your marriage. And before you say it, I know that sounds like a ton of work, but let me propose a different perspective. It's not necessarily as much about work as it is intentionality. Intimacy doesn't sustain itself; it requires consistent nurturing, effort, and understanding. I'm going to spend the next few pages doing a deep dive into ways to maintain both physical and emotional intimacy, exploring the key elements that can help keep the "blood" flowing in your marriage.

The Importance of Physical and Emotional Intimacy

Intimacy manifests itself in many ways, with physical and emotional intimacy being its two primary forms. Physical intimacy involves tangible acts of closeness such as holding hands, hugging, kissing, and sexual connection. Emotional intimacy, on the other hand, revolves around sharing thoughts, feelings, fears, and experiences. Together, they form the bedrock of a healthy relationship, each feeding into and enhancing the other. Think of physical intimacy as the oxygen component of your marriage and emotional intimacy as the nutrient component. You need both to survive, but they serve two very different purposes.

Maintaining both forms of intimacy requires ongoing communication, dedication, and a willingness to evolve as a couple. As relationships go through various phases, it becomes crucial to revisit and nurture these aspects, ensuring that they continue to serve both partners' needs and desires.

Intimacy: The Blood of Your Marriage

A significant aspect of physical intimacy is the role of sexual health and affection in maintaining a strong bond between spouses. This isn't just about the physical act of sex itself—it's about the emotional connection, vulnerability, and closeness that physical intimacy fosters. It's one of the ways couples say to each other, "I choose you, I desire you, and I want to remain connected to you." While the frequency or nature of sexual encounters may evolve over time due to life circumstances—busy schedules, health challenges, or even simply aging—it's vital for partners to intentionally prioritize this part of their relationship.

I know you may be thinking, "Girl, I'm tired, and that man wants it all the time." But here's a fact: life is always going to try to get in the way of sexy times. There are seasons when the demands of work, kids, or stress can make it feel like physical connection is just another item on an already-too-long to-do list. But intimacy shouldn't be something that gets pushed aside until "everything else is done." It needs to be cultivated and nurtured, even when life feels chaotic. Physical intimacy isn't just a bonus in a marriage—it's a fundamental part of the connection between spouses. Neglecting it for too long can create emotional distance, even if you don't realize it right away.

That's why it's so important to be intentional about making space for intimacy. This doesn't mean everything has to be spontaneous or perfect—sometimes, it means planning time together. While scheduling intimacy might not sound romantic, it's often a practical way to ensure that this important part of your relationship doesn't fall by the wayside. Think of it as prioritizing quality time in a way that nourishes your bond and strengthens your emotional connection.

Over time, the nature of your sexual relationship will likely shift, and that's completely normal. The excitement and intensity of early marriage may give way to a more comfortable rhythm, and physical intimacy may look different at 50 than it did at 25. That doesn't mean your sex life should become mundane or boring—if anything, it should become more intense as you grow together. It's a reflection of the trust, love, and commitment you've built, and it can become an even richer and more fulfilling aspect of your relationship.

Of course, changes in life circumstances—like having children, health issues, or aging—can also affect the frequency and nature of physical intimacy. These moments require grace and adaptability. Rather than focusing on what's "normal" or comparing your marriage to others, it's more important to focus on what feels right for both of you in your current season of life. Open communication about these changes is crucial. Be honest with your spouse about how you're feeling, what you need, and what's working or not working for you. These conversations can feel awkward at first, but they're essential for maintaining intimacy and keeping the connection strong.

Sexual health also plays a critical role in intimacy, and it's an area that often gets overlooked in conversations about marriage. Regular checkups, addressing any physical challenges, and staying informed about your body's needs are all important. If physical issues arise that make intimacy difficult, whether it's hormonal changes, pain, or something else, make a doctor's appointment! There is nothing to be ashamed about, and your doctor has probably already heard it all. So many couples suffer in the bedroom because of untreated medical conditions, imbalanced hormones, and other conditions your doctor can help you address. Ignoring these issues doesn't make them go away. Instead, ignoring them can lead to one or both of you feeling unwanted, rejected, frustrated, and distant. However, addressing them together can be an opportunity to deepen your trust and vulnerability with your spouse. Which leads us right into emotional intimacy.

Yes, you need to connect physically as often as possible, but a physical connection without emotional intimacy is a recipe for disaster in marriage. Both types of intimacy are vital to the sustainment and success of your relationship. While physical intimacy requires little more than attraction, emotional intimacy requires trust and vulnerability which is built over time. This is why you often hear couples say they love each other more than the day they got married. Every time you show up for each other emotionally, listen to your spouse vent about their day, hold them as they cry, or just actively be present in the moment, you are communicating that you love your spouse and value their experience and time. This builds a case for your spouse to trust you and open up to you, which also leads to deeper intimacy.

The more emotionally intimate you and your spouse are, the stronger your affection towards each other will become. Affection is what keeps the blood pumping. Sometimes, the small gestures— like holding hands, cuddling on the couch, or stealing a quick kiss in the kitchen—can be just as powerful as what happens in the bedroom. These moments of touch remind your spouse that they are loved and desired, even in the midst of a busy day. Add in a few sentiments about your positive emotions towards one another, and you've created safe space for emotional vulnerability. But remember, affection isn't just a warm-up for sex—it's a way of saying, "I see you; I value you, and I'm grateful for you."

It's also important to remember that physical intimacy isn't just about scratching an itch or responding to hormones. It's about creating an environment of safety, trust, and openness where both partners feel comfortable being vulnerable. This means being patient, listening to each other's needs, and fostering a culture of respect and care in your marriage. When intimacy is approached with love and understanding, it becomes a source of joy and connection rather than a source of stress or conflict.

At the end of the day, physical intimacy is a reflection of the love you've cultivated in your marriage. It's an opportunity to reconnect, to show affection, and to deepen the bond you share. By prioritizing this aspect of your relationship—no matter what season of life you're in—you're not just nurturing your physical connection; you're also investing in the emotional and spiritual health of your marriage.

A fulfilling sexual relationship hinges on open and honest communication. Discussing what each partner likes and dislikes can help create a space where both feel valued and respected. Avoid making assumptions about what your partner wants; instead, ask them directly and be honest about what you are willing to do. If he wants whips and chains and you are a vanilla type of girl, a much deeper conversation needs to be had! There's nothing wrong with either desire except the fact that the two of you are not on the same page. If you're grown enough to do the do, be grown enough to discuss how you enjoy doing it.

Furthermore, discussing boundaries is crucial. Each partner should feel safe expressing what they are or aren't comfortable with in their physical relationship. Building this level of comfort and trust is key to fostering a secure environment for sexual health and fulfillment. What you liked 10 years ago may not be what you enjoy today. Communicate that to your partner as well.

Physical intimacy evolves as we get older, and partners should acknowledge and adapt to these changes. Whether it's body changes, health concerns, or shifts in libido, couples should address these topics candidly. Adjustments in sexual activity don't signify a lack of desire or connection but rather an opportunity to explore new ways to express love physically. This might include exploring different forms of touch, cuddling, or non-sexual physical closeness, like holding hands or hugging. These small, everyday acts reinforce the bond between partners and serve as a reminder of their connection.

The act of touching is a powerful way to communicate love and reassurance. Studies show that physical touch releases oxytocin, the "love hormone," which helps foster a sense of trust and emotional safety between partners. Kiss each other before you leave the house and when you return. Wrap your arms around each other a few times a day, and every now and then do that thing you know sends your spouse's hormones into overdrive. Be open to doing something different! Have a staycation at a local hotel, take a spontaneous trip, plan a date night in, and enjoy a shower or bath together. It doesn't have to be expensive or fancy, but it does need to be different. Break your routine so you do not grow complacent in your intimacy.

Experimenting in the bedroom, when both partners are comfortable, can also help reignite the flame. This might mean exploring new ideas, techniques, positions, toys, or fantasies, always ensuring that both partners feel safe and respected in the process. The goal is to keep the sexual aspect of the relationship HOT! Both of your needs should be recognized and honored.

Engaging in Deep, Meaningful Conversations

In addition to physical intimacy, emotional closeness plays a vital role in nurturing a relationship. Engaging in open, meaningful conversations helps partners connect on a deeper level, fostering understanding and emotional safety. As individuals grow and change, so do their preferences and desires. Regularly discussing likes and dislikes, both in and out of the bedroom, can help ensure that each partner feels heard and valued. Whether it's about activities that bring joy, goals, or preferences in physical intimacy, these conversations help partners stay in tune with each other's needs. If you've been married longer than 5 years, you're probably not the same person you were when you got married. Make sure your spouse knows the new you.

Intimacy: The Blood of Your Marriage

Emotional intimacy thrives in an environment where both people feel safe expressing their innermost thoughts and feelings without fear of judgment or criticism. The moment you laugh when that man tells you he wants to become a rapper at 50, you totally ruin his trust. He'll never want to be vulnerable with you again. Okay, okay, that example was a little extreme, but you know I had to throw a little humor in there because I can't let this book become boring!

Anyway… when you two are discussing sensitive topics, such as sexual preferences or emotional needs, it's best to just listen actively and respond with empathy. Instead of jumping to conclusions or offering unsolicited advice, validate each other's feelings. Phrases like "I understand how you feel" or "babe, I want to support you" can go a long way in making a spouse feel seen and heard.

If you really want to take your emotional intimacy to the next level, invest in date night cards and games to help keep the conversations going without the pressure of trying to figure out what to say or ask. Then, clear your calendar a few nights a month to have real, meaningful conversations. These conversations can serve as a time to discuss how you both are feeling about the relationship, any concerns or issues that may have arisen, or anything else that you two can think of.

Another impactful way to nurture emotional intimacy is to regularly express appreciation and gratitude. It won't hurt you to tell that man how much you appreciate him, will it? Quiet as it's kept, men like words of affirmation, too! Acknowledge the small things your spouse does, from making breakfast to offering a listening ear after a tough day. Feeling appreciated reinforces the bond between partners and makes them more likely to reciprocate with acts of love and kindness.

When expressing appreciation, be specific. Instead of saying, "Thanks for everything you do," try, "Thank you for taking the trash out, the fifth time I asked." I'M JOKING!!!!! DON'T SAY THAT! A simple "Thanks for taking the trash out" will do. Just be specific so that your spouse will see that you notice what they've done and appreciate the effort they put into it.

So, remember when I said intimacy is like the blood of your marriage because it carries what you need to every area of marriage? Well, let me circle back to that analogy for a second. Have you ever felt the effects of low iron? It leaves you feeling exhausted no matter how much sleep you get. You always feel sluggish and can have trouble concentrating. Well, intimacy without honesty and transparency is like blood with low iron. It'll still flow, but if it's not corrected, you will eventually die! This doesn't mean sharing every detail of your life but being open about your feelings, needs, and experiences. For instance, if you're feeling stressed or disconnected, share this with your partner.

Look, I know you think you hide it well when something is bothering you, but the truth is your spouse can probably see and feel it. Bottling up your emotions will eventually lead to distrust because, with your mouth, you are saying you are okay, but that is a lie, and why would your spouse keep trusting someone who lies to them? I'mma let you think on that one for a second.

Intimacy: The Blood of Your Marriage

Nurturing intimacy in a relationship is an ongoing process that requires conscious effort, communication, and understanding. By prioritizing both physical and emotional intimacy, engaging in open and meaningful conversations, and building emotional safety through trust, couples can deepen their love and create a relationship that withstands the test of time, social media trends, and life's trials.

Remember, connecting with your spouse sexually is not an option; it's a requirement.

Physical intimacy, through sex and regular affection, keeps you two on the same page. Meanwhile, emotional intimacy, fostered through open dialogue, shared experiences, and mutual support, creates a foundation of trust and safety. Together, they keep the blood flowing in your marriage.

The journey of maintaining intimacy is not always easy, but it is undoubtedly one of the most beautiful and fulfilling aspects of a loving relationship. By investing in this journey together, you build a connection that not only endures but flourishes, bringing joy, comfort, and love into both of your lives.

Chapter 6:

Financial Harmony

Money. It's one of those topics that can feel uncomfortable to bring up, even with the person you've committed your life to. However, in marriage, financial harmony is one of the cornerstones of a strong relationship. Why? Because money is more than just numbers in a bank account—it's tied to our goals, values, and even our sense of security. Learning to manage it together as a team can transform not just your financial life but your marriage too.

Talking about finances isn't always easy, especially if you and your spouse have different habits, histories, or attitudes about money. But the good news is that financial harmony isn't about being perfect or agreeing on everything—it's about creating a space where you can work together, respect each other's differences, and build a plan for the future that you're both excited about. Let's dive into how to make that happen.

Discussing Financial Goals, Budgeting, and Spending Habits Openly

If there's one golden rule for financial harmony in marriage, it's this: talk about money. Don't let it become the elephant in the room. Open, honest conversations about finances create the foundation for trust and teamwork in your relationship.

Start by setting aside time to talk about your financial goals. These conversations shouldn't be one-offs—they're ongoing. Your goals as newlyweds may look very different from your goals ten years down the road. Maybe right now, you're focused on paying off debt, saving for a home, or creating an emergency fund. Later, you might be planning for kids, vacations, or retirement. Whatever stage you're in, the key is to dream together. Ask each other: What do we want our life to look like in the next five, ten, or even twenty years? What are our priorities? When you dream together, you align your hearts and set the stage for practical planning.

Once you've established your goals, it's time to dive into the details—yes, we're talking about budgeting. Now, I know budgeting doesn't sound glamorous, but it's the roadmap that turns your financial dreams into reality. The beauty of a budget is that it puts you in control. Instead of wondering where your money went, you get to tell it where to go. And the best part? You're doing this together.

A practical tool that many couples find helpful is a **budget journal**. A budget journal isn't just a list of numbers; it's a space to document your goals, track your spending, and reflect on your progress. Think of it as a financial diary for your marriage. You can include monthly expenses, savings milestones, and even little notes about what's working well and where you'd like to improve. Writing things down makes everything feel more real, and it gives you a record to look back on as you celebrate how far you've come.

When you sit down to budget, make it a team effort. Maybe one of you loves spreadsheets, and the other prefers a more visual approach—find what works for both of you. Tools like apps (such as Mint or YNAB), or even good old-fashioned pen and paper, can help you get organized. The important thing is to create a system that you'll actually use. And don't forget to build in a little flexibility. Life happens, and budgets are meant to be adjusted, not rigidly enforced.

One last note on this: be honest about your spending habits. If you're someone who loves treating yourself to coffee runs or your spouse has a habit of impulse buying gadgets, put it on the table. Talking about your habits—without judgment—gives you a chance to plan for them rather than letting them derail your budget. Honesty builds trust, and trust makes everything else easier.

Regularly Reviewing Finances Together to Avoid Misunderstandings

It's one thing to set up a budget or create financial goals, but the real magic happens when you make reviewing your finances a regular habit. Think of it like tending a garden. You can't just plant the seeds and walk away—you have to water them, pull the weeds, and watch for any signs of trouble. The same goes for your finances.

Set a regular time—whether it's once a month or every payday—to sit down together and check in on your finances. You can call it a "money date" if that makes it sound a little more fun. Light some candles, grab a cup of coffee, or even turn it into a tradition where you review your budget over takeout. The goal is to create a routine that feels approachable and stress-free.

During these check-ins, look at your budget and spending from the past month. Are you staying on track with your goals? Did any unexpected expenses pop up? Are there areas where you might want to cut back or adjust? Use this time to celebrate wins, like paying off a chunk of debt or sticking to your savings plan. Celebrating progress, no matter how small, keeps you motivated and reminds you why you're doing this.

These reviews are also a great time to bring up any concerns before they turn into misunderstandings. Money can be a sensitive subject, and it's easy for small issues to snowball if they're not addressed. For example, if one of you has been spending a little more on something than the budget allows, talk about it openly rather than letting resentment build. Approach the conversation with curiosity instead of blame—ask, "What's going on here?" rather than "Why did you do that?" This way, you're solving the problem together instead of creating conflict.

One thing to keep in mind is that these reviews aren't just about numbers. They're also a chance to check in on how you're both feeling about your finances. Is there anything causing stress or worry? Do you feel like you're making progress? Money isn't just practical—it's emotional, too, and making space for those feelings in your conversations will help you stay connected as a team.

Respecting Differences in Spending and Saving Habits

Let's be real: most couples don't come into marriage with identical financial habits. One of you might be a natural saver, while the other is more of a spender. One of you might love planning every detail of the budget, while the other prefers to take things one day at a time. And that's okay! The goal isn't to change each other—it's to understand and respect your differences while finding common ground.

Start by having an honest conversation about your financial upbringing. Did you grow up in a household where money was tight or where spending was generous? Did your parents talk openly about finances, or was it a private topic? Understanding each other's money stories can help you see where your habits come from and why you approach finances the way you do. It's not about who's "right" or "wrong"—it's about building empathy and finding ways to blend your styles.

For example, if one of you tends to save every penny while the other likes to splurge on small luxuries, create a budget that honors both perspectives. Maybe you agree to put a set percentage of your income into savings each month while also giving yourselves individual "fun money" allowances to spend however you like. This way, the saver feels secure knowing you're building your financial future, and the spender has the freedom to enjoy a little flexibility without guilt.

Another important aspect of respecting differences is giving each other grace. Nobody's perfect, and there will be times when one of you overspends or makes a financial decision the other doesn't agree with. When that happens, approach the situation with understanding rather than judgment. Remember, you're on the same team, and the goal is to move forward together.

If disagreements do arise—and they will—try to keep the big picture in mind. What are your shared goals? How can you make decisions that align with those goals while also respecting each other's individual needs and preferences? By focusing on what you're building together, you can navigate differences without letting them drive a wedge between you.

Building Financial Harmony

At the end of the day, financial harmony isn't about having a perfect budget or never making mistakes—it's about learning to work together as a team. It's about creating a financial life that reflects your shared values while also honoring your individual differences. It's about having the courage to talk openly, the discipline to plan, and the grace to give each other space to grow.

Remember, you're not just managing money—you're building a life together. Every dollar you save, every goal you set, and every challenge you overcome brings you closer to the dreams you share as a couple. When you approach finances with love, respect, and teamwork, you create a foundation of trust and security that will carry you through whatever life throws your way.

So, grab my budget journal, schedule your next money date, and start dreaming together. Because financial harmony isn't just about numbers—it's about creating a marriage where both your hearts and your goals are fully aligned.

Financial Harmony Tips

Only discuss money when you both are calm! Never, ever have discussions about your finances when you are stressed or frustrated.

As a couple, you need a strategy to discuss money. Agree on this strategy BEFORE critical financial situations arise.

Remember, you are on the same team—approach financial conversations with the proper attitude and alignment.

Create a list of your financial goals and priorities so that when it's time to talk about money, you will have an outline of the topics you want to focus on.

Budget is not a dirty word! Create a budget so you both can stay on track with your financial goals.

Remember, nothing is sexier than a couple who is saving money together!

Chapter 7:

Growing Together

"Never allow your marriage to become a sacrifice on the altar of personal ambition."

Marriage is a journey that goes beyond simply coexisting. It is a partnership where each person brings their own dreams, goals, and passions into the relationship. One of the greatest joys of marriage is the ability to grow together, supporting each other not only in your mutual goals but also in your individual pursuits. With that being said, never allow your marriage to become a sacrifice on the altar of personal ambition. We get it; you came into this thing with goals. No one wants you to abandon them. Instead, a Forever Honeymoon marriage means reaching those goals while also remembering to prioritize your spouse's goals and the needs of the marriage.

Growing together isn't just about becoming a stronger couple—it's about becoming stronger individuals who contribute to a healthier and more fulfilling partnership. Learning to navigate the balance between personal ambitions and mutual goals can lead to a more vibrant and enduring marriage. Let's explore the ways couples can grow together through personal development, shared challenges, and moments of celebration.

At the heart of any strong relationship is a foundation of support. Encouraging each other to pursue personal interests and goals is one of the most powerful ways to show love and commitment. A Forever Honeymoon doesn't require that both partners have the same dreams, but it does require that they be each other's biggest champions. Think about it: when someone goes out of their way to be your cheerleader, doesn't it make you feel loved and supported? And aren't you more likely to show up for them the same way they showed up for you? Nothing will turn a wife on like a husband who supports her dreams and goals, and the same is true for men.

When it comes to support, the phrase to remember is, "keep that same energy." I know, I know... this phrase can be used in a bad way, but in a Forever Honeymoon, we use it positively. You want support? Well, when your spouse is working on a goal, keep that same energy. Give your spouse the same support you want when you are building your dreams and achieving your goals. Never require from your spouse what you aren't willing to give. This is always going to be a two-way street.

Now, if you want to take it a step further, don't simply support what your spouse is doing with your words. Commit to understanding what drives each of you on a personal level. What are your partner's passions, hobbies, and aspirations? These may not always align perfectly with your own, and that's okay. The beauty of a strong relationship is that it allows space for each partner to explore their own identity and purpose without feeling constrained.

Make time to ask your partner about their goals. This can be as simple as, "What is something you've always wanted to achieve?" or "What's a hobby you'd like to explore more?" These conversations not only deepen your understanding of one another but also create an opportunity to express how you can support them in these endeavors. Sometimes, all it takes is a listening ear and a few words of encouragement to make a world of difference in helping your partner pursue their dreams. These conversations also build intimacy by creating a safe space for your partner to be emotionally vulnerable with you. The person you share your dreams with is the person who'll be there holding your hand when they come true.

Balancing Personal Goals with Relationship Priorities

Now, while it is essential to encourage individual growth, it's also important to maintain a balance between personal pursuits and relationship commitments. Personal ambition should never come at the expense of your relationship. Instead, finding ways to integrate both personal and mutual goals will help ensure that neither partner feels neglected nor disconnected.

For example, if one partner is working toward a career goal that requires long hours or frequent travel, it's vital to communicate openly about how this impacts the relationship and find ways to maintain a connection during busy times. So many marriages fail because of busy work and travel schedules. Then, over time, they realize they don't feel physically connected anymore. A good rule of thumb is to decide how many days you are willing to be apart. If one or both of you travel for work, sync your schedules so that you don't go beyond your agreed-upon separation time.

And here's a pro tip: Know your spouse's sex schedule. Just like every person gets hungry at different times, each person has a different number of hours or days before their body wants or needs another orgasm. If you know one or both of you are sex-everyday people, you don't need jobs or businesses that require you to be away from each other for long periods of time. If you both are once-a-week sex people, you'd probably be okay with schedules that require you to be apart for no more than 7 days. Do you see where I'm going with this? Remaining intentional about intimacy even while chasing your dreams will save your marriage IF you both are on the same page.

Supporting each other through the ebbs and flows of personal growth means understanding that there will be times when one partner's goals may take precedence for a while and other times when the focus will shift back to the relationship. Flexibility, understanding, and ongoing communication are key to maintaining harmony.

Creating a Culture of Support

One of the things I've noticed over the years on social media is a growing number of successful women citing the reason for their divorce was their husband's lack of support. While I will never judge another person's decision to end their marriage, or their reasoning to do so, I want to address the elephant in the room. Support is not a one-way street, nor is it something that one can simply demand with words. A culture of support must be developed and embraced by both members of the relationship in order for both parties to feel as though their needs are being met. Typically (I didn't say always, so stop yelling at me in your head), people are great at asking for support but can struggle when it comes to giving support to interests they are not interested in. Let me give you an example.

There's a couple who we will call DeAngelo and Lauren. They are both athletic and enjoy playing basketball. After having their first child, Lauren's interest in playing basketball has diminished. She still enjoys watching the games, but playing or attending the games just aren't fun for her anymore. DeAngelo's interest in basketball has not diminished. In fact, now that he is a father, he wants to start a nonprofit that teaches and mentors young children through the game of basketball.

Lauren sees the idea as lofty and feels she needs DeAngelo at home to help with the baby instead of trying to help other people's kids. Neither one of them is willing to budge, which leads to huge blow-up arguments. Lauren starts to resent everything associated with basketball, and DeAngelo launches his non-profit without her approval or support. He begs her to attend the games and bring their son. She refuses. This leaves Lauren at home alone with the child, who is now a toddler, three nights a week. Who's right, and who's wrong in this scenario?

If you ask me, they are both right in their feelings, passions, and viewpoints but wrong in their communication and execution. A successful marriage is not about winning an argument or only pursuing your passions. It's about finding a way to support your partner while also ensuring your needs are met. Support goes beyond just words of encouragement. It also means actively participating in or facilitating your partner's growth. This might look like giving your partner time to work on a passion project, helping them find resources or opportunities that align with their interests, or even attending events that matter to them. By showing that you are invested in their growth, you reinforce the idea that their success is also your success. If Lauren had done this, she would have avoided arguments over something DeAngelo was committed to doing.

On the other hand, DeAngelo could have explored other ways to volunteer while their child was still young so that he wouldn't have to devote so much time and energy outside of the home. He could have found someone they trusted to watch the baby one night a week to give Lauren time to get out of the house to pursue one of her passions while he was at basketball practice. This way, both of them would have had the freedom to grow individually while not neglecting their responsibilities at home.

Anytime your partner is passionate about something, make the decision to be the one who pushes them towards achieving their goals. For example, if your partner is passionate about running and training for a marathon, you might support them by attending their races, cheering them on during training, or adjusting your schedule to accommodate their workout routine. If they're working on advancing their career, you might offer to help them prepare for an important interview or discuss strategies that could help them succeed. If they launch a new business, learn what you can about the industry and offer support around the house when they need a few extra hours to get the business off the ground.

Ultimately, personal growth isn't a solo journey when you're in a relationship—it's a shared experience. When both partners are actively engaged in supporting each other's goals, it creates a culture of mutual respect and admiration, which, when executed properly, will lead to deeper intimacy.

The Power of Shared Challenges

Challenges are a natural part of life, and when faced together, they can become opportunities for growth. Whether you're navigating a financial setback, supporting each other through a health challenge, or embarking on a major life transition such as starting a family, how you handle these challenges together can define your relationship.

When couples face difficulties as a team, they develop resilience and trust. Each partner learns how to rely on the other, discovering new strengths and capabilities within themselves and their relationship. Tackling challenges together also creates a sense of unity— knowing that you have someone by your side, no matter what is incredibly empowering.

One of the most enjoyable ways to grow together is by learning something new as a couple. This could be taking a class together, learning a new hobby, or even starting a side project. The act of learning fosters a sense of curiosity and playfulness, and it can bring couples closer by creating shared experiences and memories.

For example, you might take up dancing lessons, learn how to cook a new cuisine or take on a DIY project around the house. Not only are these activities fun, but they also help couples practice patience, teamwork, and communication—skills that are vital to a healthy relationship.

Additionally, learning new things together encourages adaptability. As life evolves, the ability to grow and adapt as a couple becomes more important. Couples who are open to learning together remain flexible and willing to embrace change, which helps them navigate the twists and turns of life with greater ease.

Growth often happens outside of our comfort zones, and this is especially true for relationships. Stepping out of what feels familiar, whether it's in your personal life or as a couple, can lead to powerful growth. Taking risks together—whether big or small—can ignite new energy in your relationship.

This could involve something adventurous like traveling to a new country, trying an extreme sport, or something more personal like having deep conversations about long-term goals and aspirations. When you both step out of your comfort zones, you create opportunities for vulnerability, which strengthens emotional intimacy and trust.

Moreover, trying new things together can help break the monotony that sometimes creeps into long-term relationships. It keeps things exciting and fresh, reminding both partners of the joy that comes from discovery and growth.

Setting Mutual Goals

As much as it's important to support individual goals, having mutual goals is equally vital. Whether it's saving for a house, planning for a family, or traveling the world, setting goals together gives your relationship direction and purpose. It allows both partners to have something to work toward as a team, fostering collaboration and a sense of shared accomplishment.

Start by having regular discussions about your long-term and short-term goals. Where do you see yourselves in five or ten years? What do you want to accomplish as a couple? Once you have an idea of your mutual goals, create a plan together. This can be an exciting and motivating process, as it gives both partners a clear vision of the future they are building together.

Mutual goals don't have to be grand or life-altering—they can be as simple as deciding to spend more quality time together, planning a yearly vacation, or working on a home project. The key is to create a shared vision for the future that both partners are excited about and committed to achieving. Then, when the two of you accomplish the goal, take a step back to admire your work and celebrate together!

Celebration is one of the most overlooked but essential aspects of growing together. In the hustle of daily life, it's easy to gloss over the wins, both big and small, but these moments of achievement are what give us motivation and joy. Whether it's a significant milestone or a small victory, taking the time to celebrate together can boost morale and strengthen your bond. Every time you win together, you are building core memories for your marriage. Make time to celebrate what you did together. The work and chores will still be there tomorrow. Listen, if God took the time to look at what He accomplished and admire His work, so can you!

And when it's time to celebrate a personal win for your spouse, keep the same energy you had when you celebrated a joint goal. We don't do selfish in Forever Honeymoon!!! Celebrate your spouse even if they aren't the type to want to be celebrated. This not only shows that you are paying attention to their efforts but also reinforces that you are proud of their accomplishments. Celebrating personal achievements can be as simple as telling your spouse how proud you are, a small gift, a dinner party, or a special night in the bedroom. Whatever you choose, make sure it's something that your spouse enjoys so they will recognize your effort to acknowledge their accomplishment.

Acknowledgment is powerful because it validates the hard work that went into achieving the goal. Celebrating these moments, no matter how small, also strengthens emotional intimacy. It fosters a sense of gratitude and pride in one another, which deepens your emotional and physical connection.

While major achievements deserve special recognition, don't forget the importance of celebrating everyday wins. Sometimes, simply getting through a tough day or balancing work, family, and personal time is a victory worth celebrating. This doesn't mean you need to plan an elaborate event—sometimes a heartfelt "I'm so proud of us" or a spontaneous dance in the living room is all it takes to appreciate the little things.

These small moments of celebration create an atmosphere of joy and gratitude in the relationship. They serve as reminders that, even in the midst of life's challenges, there is always something to be thankful for. Celebrating the small things consistently builds a habit of positivity and optimism, which can help sustain the relationship through tougher times.

Growing Together, Stronger Together

In the grand journey of marriage, personal and mutual growth are key to maintaining a strong and vibrant relationship. Supporting each other's interests, learning together, and celebrating your achievements create an atmosphere where both partners feel valued, loved, and encouraged to be their best selves. Growth, whether personal or shared, doesn't have to pull you apart—instead, it can be the force that brings you closer than ever.

Remember, a strong relationship is one where both partners are committed to growing not only as a couple but also as individuals. When you encourage each other's dreams, tackle challenges as a team, and celebrate the journey along the way, you create a foundation of trust, respect, and love that can withstand any of life's storms.

Listen, friend, the bottom line is this: as you two grow, there are going to be ups, downs, and everything in between. There are going to be moments where you both wonder if you even want to remain married. Marriage is not for the weak or those who give up easily. BUT, and yes, that is a BIG BUT, there's going to come a day when you have to decide whether or not you're going to stay married just to say you stayed married or if you are going to turn the honeymoon phase into a Forever Honeymoon. Yes, you get to decide. If you're going to be in this thing until "death do you part," doesn't it make sense to make sure that while you're in it, you're doing the work to ensure you enjoy it?

The truth is, those who make the decision to make the honeymoon last forever are the ones who will also make the decision to grow individually and as a couple. Growth is already hard, but growing with another person who is also on their own personal growth journey is downright ignant at times! (And yes, I meant to say ignant! That's the Ebonics coming out of me again!) Despite how tough the road may be, when you remain committed to forever, and do the work, the joy, love, and rewards you will experience will far outweigh the work. I like to think of it this way: I was going to have to grow up and mature anyway. Why not do it with the one to whom I pledged forever?

Growth Tips

Remember, your personal growth journey does not stop when you say, "I do."

Your marriage should not be a casualty of your success.

Your partner is on the growth journey with you. Consider their wants, needs, and passions when you are setting your goals.

No one person's personal goals outweigh the importance of the marriage growth goals.

Maturing means realizing and accepting accountability for your actions, especially when they hurt your partner.

Celebrate your wins together! You both WON!!!

When things don't go the way you planned, don't blame each other. Analyze what happened and decide to grow together!

Chapter 8

Dealing with Life's Challenges

"Even honeymoons have hiccups."

Life has a way of throwing curveballs when we least expect it. No matter how carefully we plan, how organized we try to be, or how much we anticipate challenges, unexpected crises seem to find their way into our lives. Whether it's health issues, job loss, struggles with kids, or any number of other difficulties, navigating these tough times can test even the strongest relationships.

But here's the thing: challenges, as difficult as they are, also offer an opportunity for growth, connection, and deeper understanding. They can bring couples closer together if handled with care, patience, and, most importantly, teamwork. Remember, you and your spouse are on the same team. You have the same end goal in mind. Always work with that man, not against him! Now… let's get into how you can support each other through all these dang challenges that are going to pop up!

It's rough out here in these streets! How we gone get through it?

Like I said earlier, the first thing you have to remember is that you are on the same team. In the words of the great Hip Hop philosopher—and by that, I mean rapper—Fabolous, "You plus me equals better math." When life is throwing lemons and making lemonade just ain't working, don't blame your spouse for the lemons. Remember, you are both trying to make the best out of a bad situation. He loves you, and you love him. Let that love lead you as you communicate about the bitter situations you are facing. The Bible says one can chase a thousand, but two can put ten thousand to flight. (Deuteronomy 32:30) This means when you fight together, your strength is multiplied beyond human understanding. You give each other strength to endure and win the battle. But, if you play the blame game, you'll end up isolating your teammate and making the battle that much worse. You'll be fighting at home and in the streets, and who wants to do that?!?!

What I want you to do instead is focus on the big picture. This situation is temporary, but this marriage is forever. Pressure can crush you, but it can also produce diamonds. Make a decision right now that whatever comes at you is going to create another diamond for your marriage. There's a reason diamonds are a girl's best friend. Yes, they are pretty, but more importantly, they are built from hard times. Wives who understand outside pressures are there to help strengthen their marriage are less likely to fall apart when trouble hits. Be the woman who leans into her husband when she's afraid, sad, or frustrated. Blaming him for things outside of his control will only cause him to become defensive and stop talking, which will lead to another round of problems. Now, can you see how the cycle works?

The very thing that was sent to break your marriage can be the thing that makes it stronger than any substance known to man. You know challenges are going to arise, so go ahead and create a plan to keep your mind in the right place so the two of you can get through them together. I know of a couple who spends their last few moments before sleep talking about how they want to tackle different scenarios together. It seems silly, but this couple has been happily married 18 years now and has seen more than their fair share of ups and downs. No matter what they've faced, they were prepared because of all those late-night pillow talks about how they can win together. You know the saying, to fail to plan is the plan to fail. This couple planned to succeed because they had talked about potential doom before it hit. Then, when it hit, they locked hands, remembered all those late-night conversations, and weathered the storms together.

If you and your spouse are not big late-night cuddlers, consider setting coffee dates so the two of you can talk in a relaxed setting about your future and strategize on how to overcome the challenges being thrown at you. If coffee is not your jam, go to a wine bar or cigar lounge… basically, do something that relaxes you both as you make a plan. Work together to ensure what you have is rock solid!

In sickness and in health look like this?!?!

Health issues, whether they are long-term illnesses, injuries, or even mental health struggles, can be some of the most challenging crises couples face. When one partner is dealing with health concerns, it's easy for the relationship to become strained—on both sides. The person who is ill may feel vulnerable, frustrated, or even guilty for being a "burden," while the other partner might feel helpless, worried, or overwhelmed by their caregiver role.

The key here is to remember that you are in this together. If you're the one struggling with a health issue, it's important to communicate your needs clearly but also understand that your partner may not always know how to help. Sometimes, they may not get it right, and that's okay. Be patient and express your needs openly, but also give them grace as they navigate their own feelings.

For the partner who is offering support, the most valuable thing you can do is simply be there. Sometimes, that means doing practical things—like helping with doctor's appointments, managing medications, or taking over some of the household duties—but other times, it's about providing emotional support. Listen without trying to "fix" the problem. Let your partner express their fears, frustrations, and anxieties, and be a comforting presence, even if you don't have all the answers.

And remember to take care of yourself too. Caregiving is emotionally and physically draining, so it's essential to make time for your own well-being. Whether that's taking a walk, spending time with friends, or even seeking support from a counselor or therapist, you need space to recharge so that you can continue to offer the support your partner needs.

For Richer, For Poorer?

Job loss and financial struggles are incredibly stressful for any couple. Money can be one of the most significant sources of tension in a relationship, and when one or both partners are dealing with unemployment or a sudden financial crisis, that stress can feel unbearable.

If your partner has lost their job, it's easy for feelings of insecurity or inadequacy to take root. They might feel like they've let the family down or that they're failing as a provider. This is where your support can make all the difference. Let them know that you are in this together and that their worth is not tied to their paycheck. Encourage them to see this time as an opportunity to explore new career paths or consider what might bring them more fulfillment in the long run.

On the practical side, this is a good time to come together and review your finances. Sit down and take a hard look at the budget. What can you cut back on? Where can you save? How can you stretch your resources during this time? Being transparent about money, setting a plan, and making decisions together can help alleviate some of the stress that comes with financial instability.

And if you're the one facing job loss, don't be afraid to lean on your partner for support. Share your concerns and anxieties, but also trust in their love and commitment to the relationship. You are not alone, and this phase, like all others, will eventually pass.

Parenting children together is not for the weak!

Raising children brings its own set of challenges; I already told you it almost cost me my marriage. Kids are wonderful, of course, but let's be real—parenting is tough! There will be moments of joy, yes, but also times of confusion, stress, and even disagreement. How you handle these parenting struggles as a couple will shape not only your relationship with each other but also the family dynamics as a whole.

One of the biggest lessons in navigating parenting struggles is understanding that your partner's relationship with the kids is **their** relationship. This is a hard lesson to learn for many couples because it's easy to want to control or be involved in every aspect of parenting. But here's the truth: your spouse's relationship with your children is their own, separate from your relationship with them. And that's perfectly okay.

As long as their relationship with the kids isn't harmful or detrimental to the children's well-being, it's important to allow them to develop their bond without interference. This means you don't need to know every detail of every conversation or every interaction. Trust that your partner is building their relationship with the kids in their own way, and respect the boundaries of that relationship.

Of course, this doesn't mean you shouldn't have discussions about parenting styles, rules, or discipline methods. It's important to be on the same page about how you'll handle big issues as a team. But when it comes to the day-to-day, try to let go of micromanaging or controlling how your spouse parents. Trust that they love the children just as much as you do and have their own unique way of nurturing that relationship.

When you hit bumps in the road—whether it's dealing with behavioral issues, schooling challenges, or just the day-to-day stress of parenting—it's important to come together as a team. Be each other's sounding board. Share your frustrations and your wins. And when things get tough, remind yourselves that you're in this together, doing the best you can for your family.

His Relationship with the Kids is His Relationship with the Kids

One of the most transformative realizations in any partnership, especially when children are involved, is understanding and respecting that the relationship your partner has with your children is uniquely their own. Lord knows I understand how difficult it can be, especially if you're a parent who tends to want to be hands-on in every aspect of child-rearing. But here's the thing: your partner needs space to cultivate their own bond with the kids, and sometimes, that means you need to find some business to tend to so you can stay out of theirs! Yes, I said, so pick your jaw up and keep reading!

Let's be clear: this doesn't mean turning a blind eye to behavior that could be harmful. If something is truly detrimental to your children's well-being, it's absolutely your responsibility to step in. But barring that, it's important to respect the fact that your partner's relationship with your children is separate from your own.

Why is this so crucial? Because when you trust your partner to develop their own dynamic with the kids, it strengthens both their bond and your relationship. It shows that you have confidence in their parenting, and it allows for a diversity of relationships within the family. Your children benefit from seeing that both of their parents have something unique to offer.

It's also freeing for you. You don't have to manage every aspect of parenting, which gives you more room to focus on your own relationship with the kids and your spouse. In the end, trusting your partner in this way fosters a healthier family dynamic.

Sometimes, no matter how strong a couple is, external support is necessary. Whether you're dealing with mental health issues, ongoing relationship struggles, or parenting challenges, there's absolutely no shame in seeking help from outside sources. In fact, it's a sign of strength to recognize when you need additional support.

The Power of Therapy and Counseling

I'm going to keep this part super short! Girl, go find you a professional to talk to!!! (Yes, that was intentional Ebonics again.)

I am team Jesus + Therapy, so here's my two cents: whether you're dealing with deep-rooted issues or just need help navigating a specific crisis, you need someone to give you tools, wisdom, and tips to help you get to the other side. You don't know everything, so ask God to lead you to the people who have your answers in their mouths.

And while we're here, couples therapy isn't just for marriages that are "in trouble." It can be incredibly beneficial for anyone who wants to improve communication, resolve conflicts, or deepen their emotional intimacy. Sometimes, just having a neutral third party guide your conversations can help you both gain new insights into your relationship.

If you're dealing with mental health challenges, whether it's depression, anxiety, or trauma, individual therapy can be life-changing. Supporting your partner through a mental health struggle is one of the hardest things you can do, and having a therapist to guide both you and your partner can make the process more manageable.

Turning to Clergy or Religious Counseling

Now, readers, I do not know your religious beliefs or backgrounds. I am a Christian, so I want to make it clear that what I am about to share comes from my Christian beliefs and experiences. If you have differing beliefs, that's fine, but I needed to include this disclaimer so we can remain friends after you read this. If God is a part of your life and marriage, seeking counsel from a pastor or spiritual leader can be an invaluable source of guidance and strength during difficult times. God has placed spiritual leaders in our lives to offer wisdom, biblical insight, and prayerful support. When facing challenges in your marriage—whether they are related to communication, family dynamics, or personal struggles—turning to someone who can provide godly counsel can help you navigate those difficulties in a way that honors God and strengthens your faith.

Proverbs 11:14 reminds us, "Where there is no guidance, a people falls, but in an abundance of counselors there is safety." Seeking spiritual counseling from a pastor or trusted Christian leader not only reinforces the biblical values that are central to your marriage, but it also provides a Christ-centered perspective on how to handle life's challenges. Many couples find that this kind of support helps them not only grow closer to each other but also deepens their relationship with God. Spiritual counseling can be a powerful way to realign your hearts with God's will, find clarity, and restore peace in your relationship.

Whether it's advice on how to communicate better, support during a family crisis, or encouragement in your walk with Christ, seeking counsel from a trusted spiritual leader can offer both the practical tools and the prayerful support needed to get through tough seasons.

Focusing on Teamwork and Resilience

I know I've said this a few times, but I'm saying it again because I need you to get it. In the face of life's challenges, one of the most powerful things a couple can do is remember that they are a team. Being a team doesn't just mean sharing a life together—it means intentionally working together, especially when life gets difficult. Challenges, by their nature, can create stress and make us feel isolated, even when we're in a relationship. This is because we sometimes face problems that feel too personal, too overwhelming, or too heavy to share. But in a strong partnership, you never have to face these difficulties alone.

When couples approach challenges with a mindset rooted in teamwork and resilience, it's not just about surviving tough times; it's about using those experiences to come out stronger on the other side. It's about learning to lean on each other, support each other, and grow together through whatever life throws your way. Let's dive deeper into how focusing on teamwork and resilience can transform how you and your partner handle life's toughest moments.

Teamwork sounds great and all, but what does that really look like?

At its core, teamwork in a relationship means that you and your partner are aligned in your goals and your efforts. You're both working toward the same outcomes, whether that's solving a specific problem, supporting each other's individual growth, or simply getting through a stressful period. But teamwork doesn't happen automatically—it requires communication, collaboration, and a shared sense of purpose.

Here are a few ways teamwork can manifest in a relationship:

1. Open Communication:

Have you ever noticed how much basketball players talk to their teammates during practice? They are typically very vocal about when they are open, when they want the ball passed to them, and when they see their teammate score. Communication can work the same way in your marriage. Your spouse won't know you're open and able to catch the ball when passed if you don't open up your mouth and say so. On the other hand, if you need help, you also have to tell your spouse when you need them to come through with the assist. This doesn't mean dumping all of your stress on them, but it does mean keeping them in the loop so that you can tackle the issues together.

Communication also involves actively listening to your partner. When they share their thoughts or concerns, make sure you're truly hearing them—without jumping to conclusions or offering solutions before understanding the full picture. Sometimes, simply being a sounding board for your partner is one of the most effective ways to show you're in this together.

2. Sharing the Load:

Teamwork often means redistributing responsibilities when one partner is overwhelmed. If your partner is dealing with a demanding job, health issues, or family stress, you may need to step up in other areas—whether that's handling more of the household tasks, offering emotional support, or helping manage other obligations.

This isn't about keeping score. Instead, it's about recognizing when your partner needs extra help and being willing to step in, knowing that there will be times when they'll do the same for you.

When both partners feel supported and know that they can rely on each other, it creates a sense of balance in the relationship. Each person feels valued and understood, which reinforces the partnership as a whole.

3. Problem Solving Together:

When faced with a challenge, whether it's a financial crisis, a parenting struggle, or something else, teamwork involves solving the problem as a unit. This means taking time to discuss possible solutions, weighing the pros and cons, and coming up with a plan that you both feel comfortable with. It's about compromise and collaboration, not one person making all the decisions or taking on all the responsibility.

By working together to find solutions, you also reinforce your bond as a couple. Problem-solving together allows you to practice patience, empathy, and trust, which are all essential components of a healthy relationship. Even when the solution isn't perfect, or the problem persists, knowing that you're tackling it together can make a huge difference in how you both experience the challenge.

4. Mutual Encouragement:

Teamwork isn't just about the big tasks or solving problems—it's also about offering ongoing encouragement. When your partner is feeling down, stressed, or uncertain, sometimes the most powerful thing you can do is offer a few words of support. A simple "I believe in you" or "We'll get through this together" can go a long way in boosting morale and reaffirming your commitment to one another.

Mutual encouragement also means celebrating each other's strengths and recognizing the efforts your partner is putting in— even during tough times. Showing appreciation for what your partner brings to the team strengthens the bond between you and fosters a sense of gratitude, which can help both partners stay connected and motivated.

Strengthening Your Marriage Through Resilience

Building resilience in your marriage isn't just about getting through tough times—it's about coming out on the other side with a stronger bond. When couples face challenges together and learn how to support each other, solve problems, and adapt to new circumstances, it creates a deeper sense of trust and commitment. In short, facing challenges together is proof that we both meant it when we said, "for better or for worse."

Each challenge you overcome together reinforces the idea that you can rely on each other, no matter what. It strengthens the foundation of your relationship and gives you the confidence to face future challenges with greater ease. And because resilience is something that grows over time, the more you practice it, the stronger you'll become as a couple.

At the heart of both teamwork and resilience is the concept of a "we" mentality. This means seeing yourselves as a united front, always working toward the same goal. Instead of approaching challenges as individual problems, you approach them as something that affects both of you equally. It's about shifting your mindset from "me" to "we."

This "we" mentality doesn't mean you lose your individuality, but it does mean that you're always considering how your actions, decisions, and responses impact your partner and your relationship as a whole. It's a mindset that prioritizes the relationship and sees each challenge as something that both partners will work through together.

When you embrace a "we" mentality, it also makes it easier to forgive each other when mistakes are made. You start to see mistakes as opportunities for growth rather than reasons to assign blame. It fosters a sense of unity and shared responsibility, which ultimately strengthens the resilience of your relationship.

Teamwork and resilience are two of the most powerful tools you and your partner can use to navigate life's challenges. When you approach tough times as a united front—communicating openly, supporting each other, and working together—you turn challenges into opportunities for growth. By building resilience, you create a relationship that not only withstands difficulties but thrives because of them.

THE HARD TIMES CAME TO MAKE YOUR MARRIAGE STRONGER.

In the end, it's not about avoiding challenges or pretending they don't exist—it's about facing them head-on together. Through teamwork, patience, and adaptability, you and your partner can handle whatever life throws your way, confident in the knowledge that you are stronger together. Your marriage is a lifetime commitment to being two halves of the same whole. During stressful times, it's important to fight together. Instead of letting difficulties drive a wedge between you, see them as an opportunity to work as a team.

When facing a crisis, start by communicating openly. What's the issue? How does each partner feel about it? What solutions can you come up with together? By brainstorming as a team and listening to each other's perspectives, you'll find that many problems are easier to tackle when you're working together.

Also, share responsibilities. If one partner is dealing with a particularly tough issue—say, job loss—then the other partner might take on more household duties temporarily. Or, if one partner is caring for an aging parent, the other might provide emotional support and take on more of the day-to-day family tasks. Teamwork isn't about dividing everything 50/50 all the time; it's about giving whatever you need to give to ensure your marriage is at 100. Some days, you may have 20% to give. Others, you may be able to give the full 100%. Either way, a Forever Honeymoon marriage means you both are committed to doing and giving whatever is needed!

Chapter 9:

Building Traditions

"I know your Mama did it this way, but how are we going to do it?"

The Holidays are often referred to as the most wonderful time of the year. When I hear this, I wonder if it's actually wonderful or if Hallmark and other celebration-themed companies have just done an excellent job of convincing us the fights with our in-laws didn't happen, the credit card bill isn't sky high, and we didn't spend our anniversary mad at each other because one or both of us forgot what day it was.

Every marriage is different because what works for each couple is different. These differences are not omitted from the holidays. One of you may have grown up with two parents in the home who made each holiday extra special, while the other may have grown up in a single-parent home with barely enough money to get by, so holidays were never anything special to look forward to. This, of course, will mean different expectations based on your childhood experiences. Like with any difference that has not been discussed and dissected, this can lead to arguments and frustration. This is why it is imperative to make your own traditions and set expectations together regarding holidays and special dates in your marriage.

Ah, the holidays—the so-called "most wonderful time of the year." It's a magical phrase, isn't it? But if we're being honest, sometimes it feels like Hallmark and every celebration-themed company out there have done a masterful job of airbrushing reality. We're supposed to envision a perfect scene: cozy fireplaces, laughter around the dinner table, and heartwarming moments of connection. And yet, for many of us, the reality includes squabbles with in-laws, budgets stretched too thin, and, let's face it, the occasional missed anniversary that turns into a silent standoff.

Here's the truth: every marriage is different because every couple is different. What works for one relationship might feel completely wrong for another. The same holds true for how we approach holidays and special occasions. Maybe you come from a family where every holiday was an elaborate affair—stockings filled to the brim, themed breakfasts, and family photos in matching pajamas. Meanwhile, your spouse might have grown up in a single-parent home where holidays weren't much of a celebration because there wasn't enough time or money to make a big fuss. These differing backgrounds can lead to conflicting expectations, especially if you haven't had a real conversation about what holidays and special days mean to each of you.

That's why building your own traditions as a couple is so important. Creating something new together doesn't just avoid unnecessary arguments—it allows you to establish a rhythm for your relationship that reflects who you are as a team. Traditions aren't just about big events or holidays, either. They're about the little rituals and moments that weave connection into the fabric of your daily life. Let's talk about how you can build traditions that don't just make holidays more meaningful but also strengthen your marriage every single day.

Starting Small: Daily or Weekly Traditions

When we think about traditions, we often picture grand, once-a-year occasions. But the truth is, the most meaningful traditions are often the ones we practice daily or weekly. These small, consistent actions create a sense of stability and belonging in your marriage, especially during seasons when life feels unpredictable or overwhelming.

Maybe it's a weekly ritual like "Friday Night Pizza and Movie Night," where you both kick off your shoes, put on your coziest pajamas, and unwind after a long week. Or, it could be something as simple as a daily cup of coffee together in the morning before the chaos of the day begins. These little moments become anchors in your relationship, reminding you that no matter how busy life gets, you're in this together.

One of our daily traditions for my husband and me is sharing one thing we're grateful for before bed. Some nights, it's a big thing, like a new job opportunity or a meaningful conversation we had. Other nights, it's something small and silly, like being grateful for a warm blanket or the fact that we didn't burn dinner. But no matter what it is, this practice reminds us to pause, reflect, and appreciate each other. It's a way of saying, "Hey, even on the hard days, there's good in our life—and I see it because I see you."

Creating these kinds of traditions doesn't have to be complicated. Start by asking each other: What are the small moments in our day that already feel special? How can we make them more intentional? The key is to be consistent. Over time, these little rituals become the threads that weave your relationship tighter and tighter.

Making Holidays Truly "Yours"

Holidays often come with a lot of pressure. There's this unspoken expectation to meet some idealized standard of celebration—perfect decorations, endless gift-giving, and big family gatherings that feel like scenes from a holiday movie. But here's the thing: the holidays don't have to look like anyone else's. The only people who get a say in what your holidays should look like are you and your spouse.

The first step is to have an honest conversation about what holidays mean to each of you. Talk about your childhood experiences and how they shaped your expectations. What did you love about how your family celebrated? What do you want to do differently? For example, if one of you loves elaborate holiday dinners and the other feels stressed at the thought of cooking for a crowd, you might compromise by hosting a simpler gathering or alternating years.

Once you've talked about your expectations, start brainstorming your own traditions. Maybe it's baking cookies together every Christmas Eve or volunteering as a couple during Thanksgiving. Maybe it's celebrating New Year's Day with a long hike and time to reflect on your goals for the year. Whatever you choose, the point is to create something that feels meaningful to both of you—not just a copy-and-paste version of what everyone else is doing.

And don't forget to manage your stress. It's easy to let the pressure of the holidays turn something joyful into something exhausting. Give yourselves permission to say "no" to traditions that don't serve you anymore, whether it's attending a stressful family gathering or spending beyond your budget just to keep up appearances. Remember, your marriage comes first.

Anniversary Celebrations

Let's talk about anniversaries for a minute. These are the milestones that mark the passage of time in your marriage—the moments when you get to pause and celebrate all that you've built together. But let's be honest: sometimes, anniversaries can sneak up on you. Life gets busy, and before you know it, you're scrambling to find a dinner reservation or buy a last-minute gift.

That's why it's so helpful to plan ahead and create anniversary traditions that you can look forward to every year. These traditions don't have to be extravagant. In fact, some of the most meaningful ones are simple. Maybe you write each other heartfelt letters every year, reflecting on the highs and lows of the past twelve months. Or maybe you revisit the spot where you had your first date or take a yearly photo to document how your love has grown.

One couple I know spends their anniversary making a vision board together. They sit down with magazines, scissors, and glue and create a collage of their hopes and dreams for the next year of their marriage. It's a fun, creative way to reconnect and set goals as a team.

Another idea is to create a "love jar." Throughout the year, write little notes to each other about things you appreciate or special memories you've shared. On your anniversary, take turns reading the notes out loud. It's a beautiful way to reflect on the moments that made the year special.

The point is to make your anniversary about more than just dinner and flowers (though those are nice too). It's about taking time to honor your journey and recommit to the adventure ahead.

The Power of Gratitude

If there's one tradition I think every couple should adopt, it's the practice of gratitude. Gratitude has a way of shifting your perspective, even on the hardest days. It reminds you to focus on what's good, rather than what's lacking, and it keeps you grounded in appreciation for each other.

One way to incorporate gratitude into your marriage is to create a weekly gratitude practice. Maybe every Sunday evening, you sit down together and share three things you're grateful for from the past week. Or you could keep a gratitude journal as a couple, writing down the blessings you've experienced and the ways you've seen God at work in your lives.

Gratitude can also be woven into your daily life. Start each morning by thanking God for your spouse and asking Him to bless your marriage. Leave little notes of appreciation for your partner—on the bathroom mirror, in their lunchbox, or tucked into their wallet. These small gestures may seem insignificant, but they have a way of building connection and reminding your spouse that they're seen, valued, and loved.

Over time, gratitude becomes a lens through which you see your marriage. Instead of focusing on the things that annoy you or the ways your spouse falls short, you start to notice the little things they do right—the kindness, the effort, and the love they show in their own unique way. And that shift in perspective can transform your relationship.

Traditions as a Foundation

At the end of the day, traditions aren't just about the activities themselves. They're about what those activities represent—your commitment to each other, your shared memories, and the love that grows deeper with each passing year. Traditions are the foundation of a thriving marriage, not because they're perfect, but because they're intentional.

So, start small. Choose one or two traditions to begin with, and let them grow over time. Be flexible, and don't be afraid to adjust your traditions as your marriage evolves. The goal isn't perfection—it's connection.

And remember, every tradition you create together is a thread in the tapestry of your love story. Whether it's a daily ritual, a holiday tradition, or a special anniversary celebration, these moments are the building blocks of a marriage that's strong, joyful, and uniquely yours.

Your marriage deserves to be celebrated—not just on the big days, but every single day. So go ahead, build those traditions. Make them your own. And watch as they transform your relationship into something even more beautiful than you ever imagined.

Chapter 10:

Beyond Love — Deepening Connection

Transitioning from a Honeymoon Phase to a Forever Honeymoon

"Marriage brings power, protection, and provision." -**Tomeka Lynch Purcell.**

All interpersonal relationships require work. The fact is, humans are some of the most "interesting" creatures God created. Yes, interesting is my adjective of choice because I don't want to be offensive to God about His children. But you've met them, and by them, I mean people in general, so I know you know what I'm saying! All humans can be "interesting" depending on the time of day, what's going on in their mental and emotional health, their culture, and a host of other variables. This means being in any type of relationship with another human can be difficult at times. Why is it, then, that marriage gets a bad reputation? No one is saying "sistering" is hard. (Yes, I made that word up... just go with it.) But, when it comes to marriage, no one wants to discuss the benefits. Everyone screams and records podcasts about how difficult it is. What about the power, protection, and provision marriage brings?

Listen, being married and being in a committed relationship is a BEAUTIFUL thing! Stop letting people lie to you. Stop accepting the past trauma and disappointment of others shape your opinion and perception of marriage. Nothing is better than having your best friend, protector, lover, and soul mate in your life. There is nothing better than having someone to come home to at the end of the day to celebrate your wins with you or encourage you after a rough day.

Marriage is a sacred and beautiful lifelong commitment that does not need to be described based on the difficult days. It is far more beneficial and emotionally sane to focus on the positive attributes marriage brings into your life. As you and your spouse grow in all of the areas we've discussed so far, my prayer for you is that your focus shifts from what is wrong in your relationship to all the things that are right. I pray you begin to celebrate and magnify the good you and your spouse experience daily. I pray your deepening communication leads to a more seasoned love, one that is full of companionate love, commitment, kindness, and thoughtfulness. You and your spouse both deserve to experience this. I want to break down this deepening connection to help you understand what it is and how it can be developed in your marriage.

Transitioning love: From passionate to companionate love.

Let me be SUPER clear right now. Don't let the title of this section fool you. As your love deepens and grows from hot and heavy to deep and weighty, the spice does not need to die down in your marriage. In fact, it's the opposite. As you grow deeper and deeper in love with your spouse, the passion grows because what's more attractive than the one who's held you down in the thick of it?

BUT!!! The deeper your love grows, the more compassionate you will become towards your spouse.

Compassionate love does not replace passionate love; it builds upon it. This type of love always prioritizes the health and well-being of your spouse ahead of yourself. You may be wondering how your needs will be met if you always put your spouse first. It's simple. Your needs will be met because true, compassionate love is reciprocated. Your spouse will be putting your needs first as well. Compassionate love is full of action, support, tenderness, and a deep yearning to make life better for the one you love.

Compassionate love will support you through Cancer treatments and bankruptcy. It will stand in front of you on the battlefield and take every bullet just to keep you from feeling a moment of pain. When you transition to compassionate love, you are ready to turn your honeymoon phase into a Forever Honeymoon!

Keep the fire, passion, and compassion going by regularly checking in with yourself and your spouse about the marriage, their needs, and your commitment to each other. Do not become lazy now that your connection is deeper than the sweaty afterglow of sex. This is the time to keep your intentionality high. Never become too complacent in your marriage. Make sure your spouse knows their needs will ALWAYS be your top priority. Even if you only have a short amount of time and a nonexistent budget, be creative in your expression of love and faithfulness to your spouse.

Everything you did to win your spouse is needed to keep your spouse. If you want to ensure your marriage won't turn out like other marriages you've seen end far too soon, make sure you are keeping the fire lit and the emotional connection on 1,000. The honeymoon should never be a week of vacation or a few days after you exchange vows. The honeymoon was always meant to last FOREVER!

Deepening Connection Action Plan

Use the space below to write an action plan to help strengthen your connection with your partner.

_____

_____

_____

_____

_____

_____

_____

_____

_____

_____

_____

_____

_____

_____

_____

_____

Chapter 11:

The Lifelong Journey

Keeping the Spark Alive

"The same amount of time and meticulous planning you dedicate to planning your wedding must be applied to staying married." -**Tomeka Lynch Purcell.**

So, you spent all the money. You took the pictures and posted so that all of social media could share in the joy of your special day. You floated on cloud 9 all the way through the honeymoon. You had dimension-bending sex that made you feel like you could swing from the chandeliers... seriously, your toes curled, and your eyes rolled into the back of your head. Now what?

What are you going to do once you get back home, and that man who seems to know your body better than you do can't remember how to put his socks in the dirty clothes hamper? What do you do when life throws stress, arguments, and unexpected challenges your way, leaving you both wondering how to navigate it all? You're going to do the same thing you did when you were planning the wedding. That's right, the same steps you took to plan the most important day of your life can help you build a marriage that's even more beautiful than your wedding. Let's break it down, step by step.

Step 1: Envision What You Want

When you were planning your wedding, the first thing you likely did was dream. You pictured the perfect dress, the flowers, the venue, the music—all the details that would make your special day unforgettable. Before anything else, you had a vision.

The same is true for marriage. You need to start by envisioning what you want your marriage to look like. Take time to dream together with your spouse. What kind of partnership do you want to build? How do you want to communicate, resolve conflicts, and support each other? What kind of legacy do you want to leave for your family? These aren't just abstract questions—they're the foundation of your life together.

Write down your vision. Make it specific. For example, you might say, "We want a marriage where we prioritize date nights, communicate openly, pray together daily, and create a home filled with laughter and peace." This vision becomes your roadmap, guiding your choices and reminding you of your shared goals when life gets tough.

But here's the key: just like your wedding vision had to accommodate your budget, venue availability, and other realities, your marriage vision has to be flexible. Life will throw curveballs, and that's okay. The important thing is that you and your spouse are committed to working toward your vision together, even when things don't go exactly as planned.

Step 2: Get Help with the Planning

If you're like most couples, you didn't plan your wedding alone. You had help—whether it was from a professional wedding planner, your family, or your bridal party. You leaned on others for support, advice, and expertise to make your vision a reality.

Marriage is no different. You don't have to figure everything out on your own. Seeking help is not a sign of weakness; it's a sign of wisdom. Surround yourself with people who want to see your marriage succeed—mentors, trusted friends, family members, or even professional counselors. These are your "planners," the people who can offer guidance when you need it most.

One of the best sources of help is a couple who has been married longer and has the kind of relationship you admire. Ask them how they navigate challenges, what keeps them connected, and what lessons they've learned along the way. Their experience can be a valuable resource as you build your own marriage.

And let's not forget God. He is the ultimate planner, the one who designed marriage, and knows exactly what you need to thrive. Don't be afraid to seek His guidance through prayer, Scripture, and the counsel of godly mentors. When you invite Him into your marriage, you're leaning on the One who sees the whole picture and can lead you through even the most challenging times.

Step 3: Create a Budget

Every wedding has a budget, whether it's a shoestring affair or an extravagant celebration. You had to decide how much to spend on the dress, the venue, the flowers, and everything else. You learned to allocate your resources wisely to make the day as beautiful as possible without going broke.

Marriage also requires a budget, but this time, it's not just about money—it's about your time, energy, and attention. You only have so much of each, and how you choose to spend them will determine the health of your marriage.

Start by budgeting your time. Make room in your schedule for your spouse, no matter how busy life gets. Date nights, regular check-ins, and even small daily rituals like having coffee together are investments in your relationship. Don't let work, kids or other responsibilities eat up all your time without leaving anything for your marriage.

Next, budget your energy. Marriage takes effort, and it's easy to feel drained when life gets overwhelming. Be intentional about taking care of yourself—physically, emotionally, and spiritually—so that you have the energy to pour into your spouse and your relationship.

And, of course, budget your money. Finances are one of the leading causes of stress in marriage, so creating a financial plan together is essential. Agree on spending priorities, set savings goals, and be transparent about your financial habits. When you manage your resources as a team, it strengthens your bond and reduces unnecessary tension.

Step 4: Trust Your Coordinator

During your wedding, you probably relied on someone—a wedding planner, a trusted friend, or a family member—to help coordinate the details. They made sure everything ran smoothly so you could focus on enjoying your special day. In marriage, you also need someone you can trust to guide you and keep things on track. That someone is God.

Trusting God as the "coordinator" of your marriage means surrendering control to Him and relying on His wisdom instead of your own. Proverbs 3:5-6 reminds us, "Trust in the Lord with all your heart and lean not on your own understanding; in all your ways submit to Him, and He will make your paths straight."

This doesn't mean you won't face challenges. But it does mean that you don't have to navigate them alone. When you put your trust in God, you're placing your marriage in the hands of the One who knows you and your spouse better than you know yourselves. Seek Him in prayer, follow His principles, and trust that He is working for your good—even when things feel uncertain.

Step 5: Delegate Duties

A successful wedding requires teamwork. You had a bridal party, family members, or friends who pitched in to help with everything from setting up the venue to organizing the guest list. You knew you couldn't do it all on your own, so you delegated.

Marriage is also a team effort. You and your spouse need to share the load—not just the physical tasks of daily life, like cooking, cleaning, and paying bills, but also the emotional and relational work that keeps your marriage strong.

Start by having honest conversations about expectations. Who will handle which responsibilities? How can you support each other's strengths and lighten each other's burdens? Remember, it's not about dividing everything 50/50—it's about doing what works best for both of you.

Delegating also means trusting your spouse to handle their responsibilities without micromanaging. Just like you wouldn't hover over your bridesmaids to make sure they're holding their bouquets correctly, you don't need to oversee every detail of your spouse's contributions. Trust them to do their part, and offer grace when things don't go perfectly.

Step 6: Pray the Rain Doesn't Ruin Your Day

No matter how much you plan, some things are beyond your control—like the weather on your wedding day. You can choose the perfect venue but can't stop the rain. The same is true in marriage. There will be storms you can't predict or prevent, and they'll test your commitment, patience, and faith.

But here's the thing: storms don't have to ruin your marriage. They can strengthen it if you face them together. When challenges come—whether it's financial struggles, health issues, or unexpected life changes—lean on each other and on God. Pray together, seek wisdom, and remember that storms don't last forever. As Ecclesiastes 4:9-10 says, "Two are better than one because they have a good return for their labor: If either of them falls down, one can help the other up."

Your wedding might have had a backup plan for rain, like an indoor venue or a tent. In marriage, your backup plan is faith and teamwork. When the rain comes, hold onto each other and trust that God is working behind the scenes to bring beauty out of the storm.

Your wedding was just the beginning. Marriage is the real journey, and like any great journey, it requires preparation, intentionality, and perseverance. By envisioning what you want, seeking help, budgeting your resources, trusting God, sharing responsibilities, and weathering storms together, you can build a marriage that's even more beautiful than the day you said, "I do."

So, breathe, Sis! You got this. Marriage isn't about perfection—it's about commitment, love, and the willingness to keep showing up, day after day. Just like your wedding, your marriage will have its share of challenges, but it will also be filled with joy, laughter, and moments that take your breath away. And when you plan with purpose, trust in God, and work together as a team, your marriage will be a testament to the love, grace, and faithfulness that brought you together in the first place.

Bonus Tips

Commit to continuous improvement and adapting. You're now in a lifelong marathon. There will be moments to sprint, but there will be more moments to slow down and pace yourself so that the journey does not become overwhelming. Just don't stop making progress. Remember, even babies can move from one place to another when they crawl. They don't move as fast as you can walk, but they make progress. Honor the crawling moments in your marriage; don't resent them.

Understand that each phase of marriage brings new challenges and joys. There is just as much joy in the golden years as there is in the child-rearing years. Be intentional about seeing the joy in every phase. Don't long for yesterday when you can create a better today, and don't salivate for tomorrow when today is already here.

Stay dedicated to each other with patience, love, and relentless effort. As we've discussed many times in this book, life is going to come at both of you fast. You will always get through it stronger, wiser, and better if you remember you're on the same side of the fight. I heard a saying: "There is one way out of this marriage, and the door ain't it." That simply means we're in this until one of us takes our last breath. We're committed to this marriage no matter what. When two people love so deeply that they remain committed to patience, love, and relentless effort, the end result will always be a Forever Honeymoon.

Give each other the grace you desire. It's so easy to want grace, but it can sometimes be difficult to give it. Grace, like love and forgiveness, is often received in the measure it is given. So, if you want grace from your spouse, you have to be willing to give grace. Today, he messed up, but tomorrow, it could be you, so think twice before you flip. Whatever you sow is going to boomerang its way back to you.

Disappointment is a sneaky thief. If you're not vigilant, you'll find yourself mad at the world when the only thing that's wrong is that last business deal didn't go the way you wanted. Instead of withdrawing from your spouse when you are disappointed, lean in. Be vulnerable and share the disappointment, even if it was your spouse that disappointed you. Allow your spouse to help you process your emotions. And P.S… a little sensual healing can go a long way in this area.

It is never too late to improve your marriage. As long as you both are still breathing and committed, your marriage can be successful. It is never too late to turn things around and save your marriage. You may have had a rough start or a rough middle, but with the right tools and implementation, today can be the beginning of your Forever Honeymoon.

Chapter 12:

7 Killers of Marriage -The Pathway to Divorce

Why on earth would I include the 7 killers of marriage at the end of a book about keeping the love and spice in your marriage? Because if you're going to preserve your marriage, you need to be aware of the things that will literally try to kill what you are fighting to nurture. The Bible says in Song of Solomon 2:15 (NLT), "Catch all the foxes, those little foxes, before they ruin the vineyard of love, for the grapevines are blossoming." In other words, this whole book has been about the things you can do to nurture the "grapevines" of your marriage. And when you put in the work, the fruit of your marriage will be plentiful. But beware, fruit attracts foxes. When the scripture says, **catch all the foxes**, it's warning you not to get so caught up in love land that you forget the best offense is a great defense! That's not just a sports or military analogy; it's a golden rule for your marriage.

Let's get into these 7 killers of marriage and how you can defend your marriage against each of them.

1. Neglect

Neglect is one of the quietest killers of marriage. It doesn't show up with flashing lights or dramatic entrances. Instead, it sneaks in slowly, like a tiny crack in the foundation that grows over time until it threatens the entire structure. It's what happens when we become complacent and stop doing the things that attracted our partner to us in the first place. Remember how you got dolled up for dates before marriage? Remember the butterflies you felt anticipating the way your spouse would look at you when the hair, makeup, and outfit were hitting just right? Remember the wax and pedicure appointments before sexy time? Yeah... all of those memories should still be present-day experiences!!!

Neglect is not always about the big things. Sometimes, we neglect our marriage when we stop prioritizing our spouse and the things we can do to please them. I don't believe neglect is intentional. It happens when the busyness of work, kids, errands, and responsibilities take over, and we unintentionally put our marriage on the back burner. When we are facing real-life expectations and responsibilities, we can wrongly believe our spouse should just understand we're busy and don't have two free hours to prepare for a date. Well, remember when we discussed realistic expectations? This is one of those times you need to have a come-to-Jesus meeting with yourself. Not neglecting your marriage has nothing to do with what your spouse understands. It's about your priorities. A happy, healthy, and loving marriage should ALWAYS be your top priority.

No matter how busy you or your spouse are, marriage requires ongoing attention. Love needs tending, like a garden. If you neglect to water it, pull the weeds, and care for the soil, it won't thrive. You may not have two hours per week for glam, but can you pre-schedule your beauty maintenance, salon/barber, or spa appointments to ensure you are doing your part to remain physically appealing to your spouse? I have a friend who says, "My man passed up a whole lot of fine out there in them streets to remain faithful to me. The least I can do is make sure when he comes home, he has something to look at that sends all his blood to his groin." I'm laughing as I type this, but she is so serious when she says it.

Neglecting to care for your appearance is the same as neglecting your marriage. Get dressed, put some makeup on, and remind that man why he fell in love in the first place. I promise it wasn't your cooking. And while we're on the subject of cooking, even though you may be extremely busy, pull that calendar out and plan a few dates at home. Cook for that man or cater his favorite meal. Get cute, and then spend some time reconnecting over dinner. And while you're at it, plan a few day dates and do some of the things the two of you did while dating. Your calendar is filled with all of the important things that require your attention, right? Then why isn't your marriage on your calendar? And if it is, that stray wasn't for you, Sis—it's for our girl over there reading this book and rolling her eyes cuz I'm stepping all over her toes. Sis has a fine man at home and won't give him none because she gives all of what she has to her work.

Now, what was I saying? Oh yeah… be intentional about your marriage. Take time to regularly check in with each other, even during busy seasons. Schedule date nights and keep them even when he gets on your nerves. It doesn't have to be expensive or fancy; it's about the two of you prioritizing your forever, and that looks different for every couple. The key is consistent effort so that you both feel loved and valued. Send that man a flirty text the next time you have a flashback of how he used to make you sweat your hair out! The way to defeat neglect is to be intentional about making the honeymoon last forever.

2. External Pressures

Baby, external pressures could be a whole book all by itself, but I'm not gonna do that to you. You've been rocking with me this whole book, so I'm not going to mess up our flow now. External pressures come in many forms: work stress, family expectations, societal demands, or even well-meaning friends who unintentionally overstep boundaries. These pressures can weigh heavily on a marriage, especially when they're not acknowledged or managed as a team. The danger lies in allowing these external forces to take priority over your relationship.

One of the best ways to combat external pressures is to protect the sanctity of your marriage. Think of your relationship as a fortress with walls that keep out anything that threatens your bond. This doesn't mean isolating yourselves from the world, but it does mean creating boundaries. For example, if work demands are taking too much of your time and energy, sit down together and discuss ways to regain balance. If the extended family has too much influence, kindly but firmly set limits.

Remember, your marriage is your first ministry. External pressures will always exist, but how you handle them together will determine whether they strengthen or weaken your bond. When you approach these challenges as a team, you show the world—and each other—that your relationship comes first.

3. Unresolved Past Issues

We all come into marriage with baggage. Whether it's from childhood, past relationships, or previous mistakes, unresolved issues can act like landmines in a marriage. If not addressed, they can explode at the worst times, causing pain and division.

The first step in dealing with unresolved issues is to recognize that they exist. Denial only delays healing. Be willing to have honest, vulnerable conversations with your spouse about the things that are weighing on your heart. Maybe it's a hurt from the past that still lingers, or maybe it's a pattern of behavior that stems from an old wound. Whatever it is, bringing it into the light is the first step toward healing.

Sometimes, resolving past issues requires outside help. Seeking counseling or pastoral guidance is not a sign of weakness—it's a sign of strength and a commitment to your marriage. Healing takes time, but when you do the work, you free your marriage from the chains of the past and allow it to flourish in the present.

4. Lack of Respect

Respect is the cornerstone of any healthy relationship. Without it, love begins to wither. Lack of respect can manifest in many ways: harsh words, dismissive attitudes, or taking your spouse for granted. Over time, these small slights can create a chasm in your marriage.

Respect in marriage means valuing your spouse's thoughts, feelings, and contributions. It means listening without interrupting, speaking without belittling, and choosing kindness even when you're frustrated. The way you speak to your spouse—and about them— matters deeply. Proverbs 15:1 reminds us, "A gentle answer turns away wrath, but a harsh word stirs up anger."

If respect has been lacking in your marriage, it's never too late to rebuild it. Start by examining your own behavior. Are there areas where you've fallen short? Apologize sincerely and commit to doing better. And when your spouse shows respect toward you, acknowledge it and reciprocate. Respect is contagious, and when both partners make it a priority, it transforms the entire relationship.

5. Lack of Intimacy

Intimacy is the glue that binds a marriage together, and it goes far beyond the physical. Emotional intimacy, spiritual intimacy, and physical intimacy are all vital to a thriving relationship. When any of these areas are neglected, it creates a disconnect that can leave both partners feeling lonely and unfulfilled.

Physical intimacy is often the first thing people think of, and while it's important, it's not the whole picture. Emotional intimacy—the ability to share your thoughts, dreams, and vulnerabilities—is just as crucial. Spiritual intimacy, the bond that comes from praying together, studying God's Word, and seeking His will for your marriage, is the foundation that supports everything else.

If intimacy has been lacking in your marriage, take small steps to rebuild it. Spend time together without distractions. Have meaningful conversations where you truly listen to each other. And don't underestimate the power of prayer—it's hard to stay distant from someone you're praying with and for. Intimacy is a journey, and it grows when both partners make an effort to nurture it.

6. Infidelity

Infidelity is one of the most painful breaches of trust in a marriage. While it's often associated with physical affairs, emotional infidelity—forming an inappropriate bond with someone outside the marriage—can be just as damaging. Infidelity doesn't happen in a vacuum; it's often the result of unmet needs, poor boundaries, or unresolved issues.

The best defense against infidelity is to guard your heart and your marriage. Proverbs 4:23 advises, "Above all else, guard your heart, for everything you do flows from it." Be intentional about protecting your relationship by setting clear boundaries with the opposite sex, staying accountable to each other, and addressing issues before they fester.

If infidelity has already occurred, healing is possible, but it takes time, effort, and a willingness to rebuild trust. Seek professional help and lean on God for guidance and strength. With His grace, even the deepest wounds can be healed.

7. Money

Money issues are one of the leading causes of stress in marriage. Whether it's overspending, differing financial goals, or simply a lack of communication, financial problems can quickly create tension and conflict.

The key to overcoming money challenges is open communication and teamwork. Sit down regularly to review your finances, set goals, and create a budget that reflects your shared priorities. Respect each other's perspectives—maybe one of you is a saver, and the other is a spender. Instead of letting these differences cause friction, use them as an opportunity to balance each other out.

Remember, your finances are a tool, not a battleground. When you approach money as a team, you're not just managing resources— you're building a future together. And as with everything else in marriage, invite God into your financial decisions. Pray for wisdom, practice stewardship, and trust Him to provide.

Your marriage is a precious gift, a vineyard that you've worked hard to cultivate. And like any vineyard, it needs protection. The seven killers we've discussed—neglect, external pressures, unresolved past issues, lack of respect, lack of intimacy, infidelity, and money—are the "foxes" that can destroy the fruit of your labor if left unchecked.

But here's the good news: with intentionality, prayer, and teamwork, you can guard your marriage against these threats. Remember, your relationship is worth fighting for. Keep nurturing the love you've built, stay vigilant against the foxes, and trust God to strengthen your bond.

As you move forward, take these words from 1 Corinthians 16:13-14 to heart: "Be on your guard; stand firm in the faith; be courageous; be strong. Do everything in love." Your marriage is a reflection of God's love, and with Him at the center, it will not only survive but thrive. Keep tending your vineyard, and may your love continue to grow and flourish for years to come.

www.ingramcontent.com/pod-product-compliance
Lightning Source LLC
Chambersburg PA
CBHW051320120626
46547CB00015B/2323